AF580357

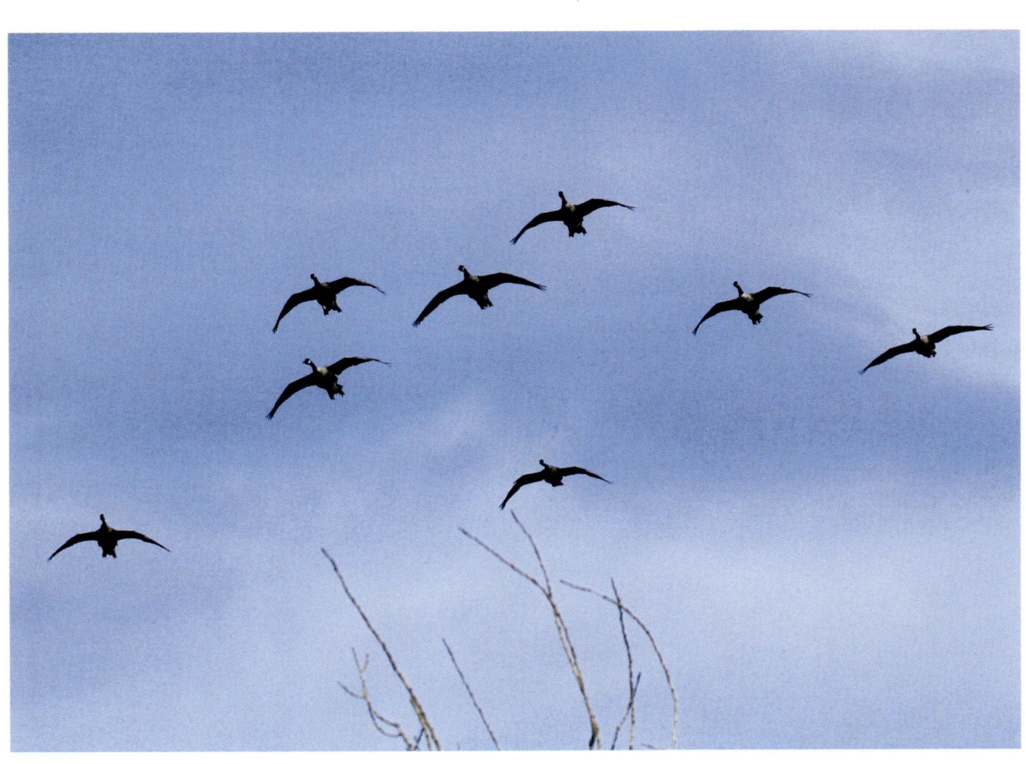

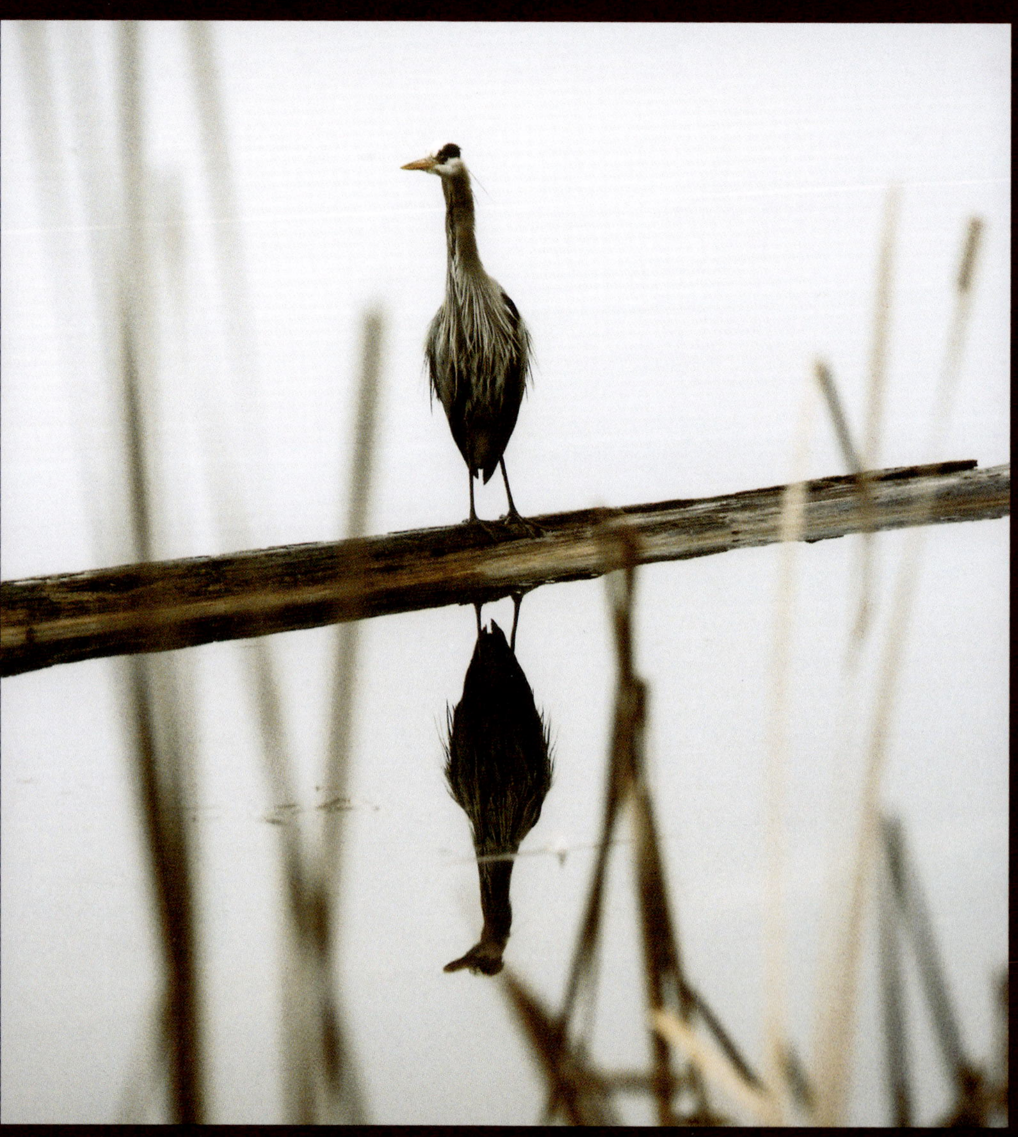

THE WILD WITHIN

WETLANDS OF THE WASHINGTON PARK ARBORETUM

Featured Photographers:

Michele A. Burton, Camden Hackworth,

Shannon Marie Sweeney, Lisa P. Anderson,

and Kevin Ebi

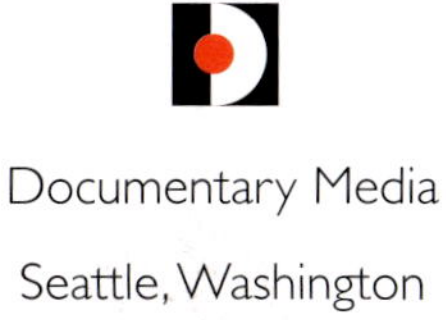

Documentary Media

Seattle, Washington

Introduction

Every day, 100,000 cars pass through Seattle's Washington Park Arboretum wetlands. And while the speed, awareness, and interest of the occupants vary, for the most part these wetlands pass by only on the edge of their consciousness. Some commuters may appreciate the wetlands' beauty as they make their stop-and-go way over the Evergreen Point Floating Bridge, between Seattle and the east side of Lake Washington. They may even notice a heron, an eagle perched on a roadside snag, or the long-standing beaver lodge on the north side of the throughway, but much of the wetlands' majesty and most of their mystery are lost to the demands of the journey.

My wife, Lisa, was born here and, as a result, had the opportunity to appreciate and acclimatize to these wetlands over many years of traveling back and forth across Lake Washington. I, on the other hand, stumbled upon them unexpectedly in one startling moment 20 years ago, the engine of my Honda Civic still hot from the 800-mile trip north from a land of chaparral and suburbs. To Lisa, the wetlands seem, perhaps, natural, like a piece of fabric in a much-loved quilt. To me, they were, and are, absurdly wonderful and improbable, like a snowstorm on the Fourth of July. To both of us, they are essential to our appreciation of Seattle and vital to our understanding of what makes this a great city.

The remarkable beauty and value of these wetlands can only be fully appreciated up close, at a slow, intimate pace. This book offers such a view. The text and images describing this urban environmental treasure were created by a cadre of talented, perceptive, and thoughtful citizens with a deep appreciation of the uniqueness within the Arboretum's shoreline boundaries. It is the express intent of these contributing citizens to share their insights on the grace, wildness, natural artistry, and surprise that exist within the wetlands, just beyond the gaze of somnambulant commuters.

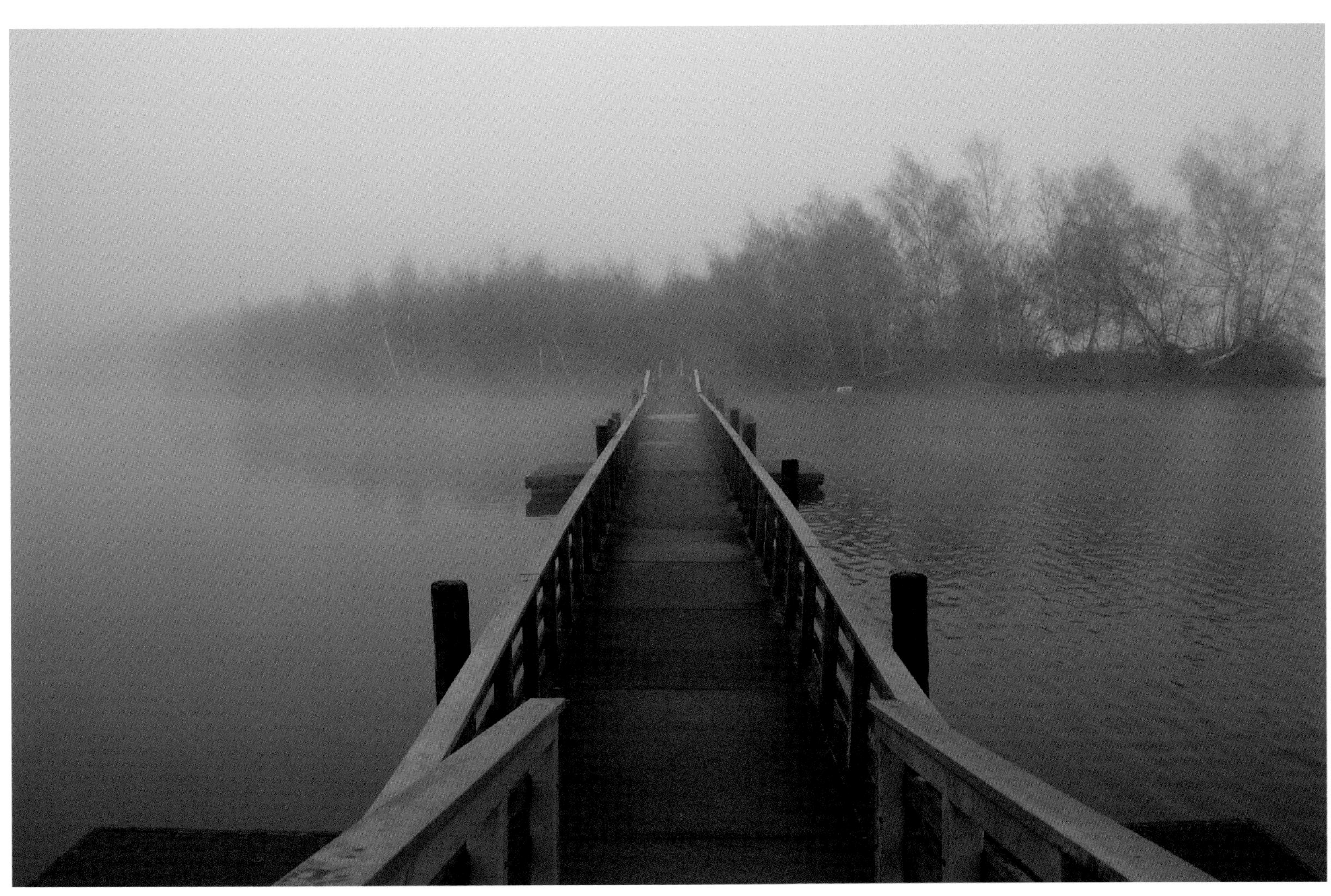

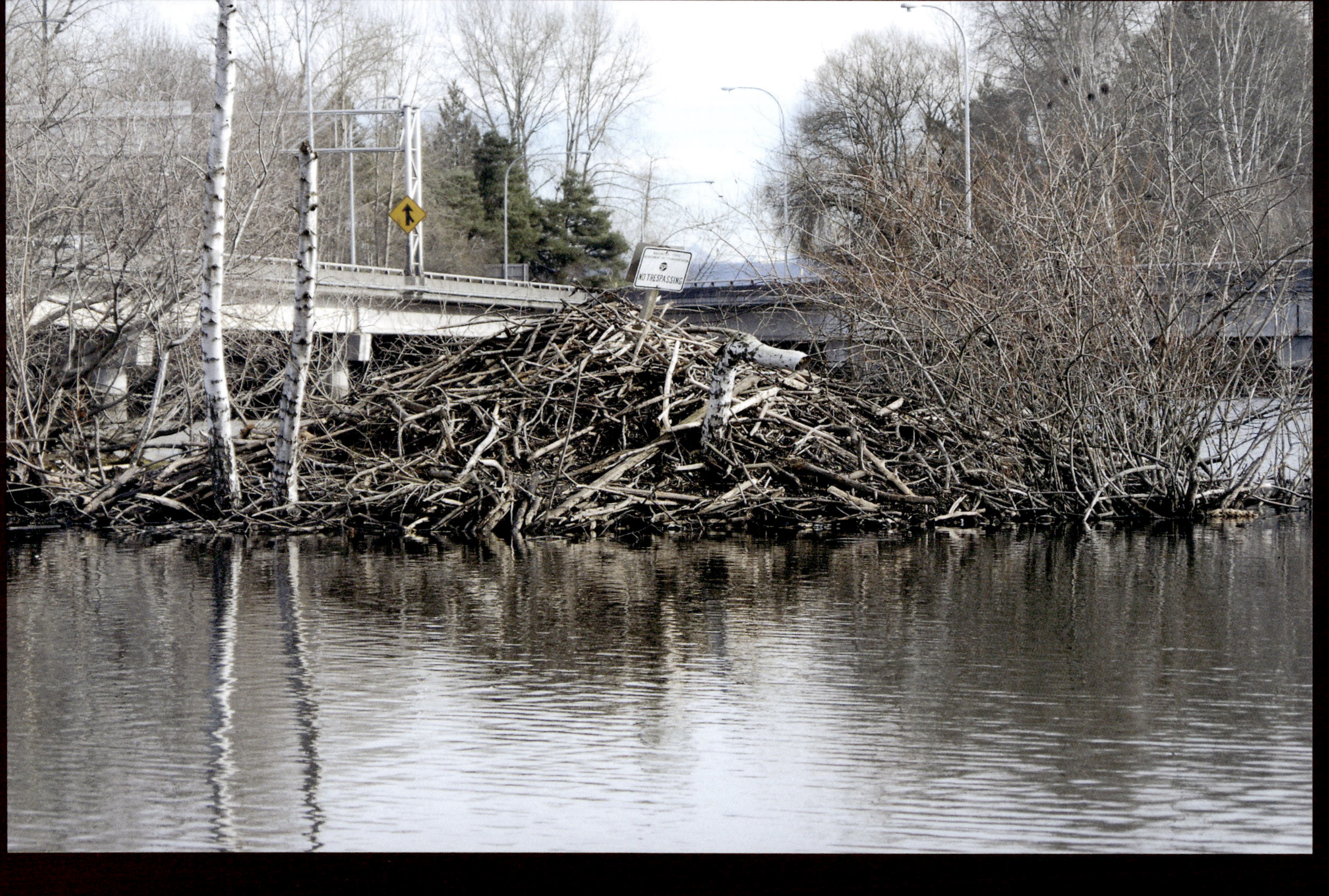
NO TRESPASSING

Today Lisa and I live and raise our children in very close proximity to these same wetlands I first ogled from the right lane of the 520 freeway so long ago. While building our home, we felt an immediate connection to our new environment as we noticed an eagle couple doing the same nearby—determinedly shuttling branches, huge branches, to a tall stand 1,000 feet from the water's edge. I startle even today at the size, speed, and strength of our eagle neighbors, feathers slicing the air above my head in a low whistle as they carefully maintain their home and feed their pre-fledgling family.

Our home's proximity to the wetlands allows us to experience them intimately, on a daily basis. At night we sometimes walk down to the water and peer into the wetlands' edge. In the distance cars pass, as always, along the freeway. Closer in, though, a different sort of traffic passes by; beavers, in calm, wakeless circles, patrol the borders of their lodge. Occasionally a thunderous warning slap, sounding like a 10-pound boulder dropped from the sky, breaks the stillness. The beavers disappear, only to resurface minutes later to resume their patrol once again.

In the winter, wood ducks arrive like chivalrous dandies, dressed to the hilt and ready to impress. Matronly coots arrive in great numbers as well and cluster in tight groups at the first sight of a raptor soaring above. Their prim, church-lady bodies busily skim the water, vigilant, as church ladies are, lest they attract the eye of the enemy-eagle overhead.

Shovelers, buffleheads, waxwings, sapsuckers all make their home here, at some point or another, while other migrants stop only briefly before taking flight. Wrens construct nests on stilts in the reeds. Canadian honker geese come and, to the dismay of some, stay. Ducklings are hatched, taught to survive, and sent on their way, this place imprinted in their mind, as in ours, forever.

Another layer reveals itself when one stops to look closely at the patterns designed by nature. Early morning sun creates a pattern of tall shadows across a snowy field, ripples of light and water traverse the lake surface, jagged cracks lace thick fingers across the trunk of a beech, and brilliant red berries set themselves against a background of fall leaves. Every season provides a new display of Nature's art, missed by casual passersby but celebrated here by those with an eye for such things.

Surprising things happen in the margins of the wetlands, too. We find crawdads dead, sprawled lifeless on the land, 100 feet from the water, and discarded oyster shells, drilled with precision accuracy, sucked dry and dropped carelessly on piles of leaves. Otters invoke squatter's rights, invading and despoiling moored boats. Turtles pull themselves up onto lawns to lay eggs. Beavers industriously make off with an entire stack of cut firewood and landscape amenities as they choose. A seal pops his head up, looking as confused as we are at his arrival. Coyotes yowl in the early morning fog. Wildness persists.

And then there are the herons, the great blues, and their smaller cousins, the green herons, patiently stalking, staring fixedly into the murky green water. They stand, beyond the point of stillness, and then strike with the speed of a snake, snatching their unsuspecting prey from the peace of the water's edge. Their flight never fails to astound—an unlikely orchestration of bone and wing and feather—as if a building in mid-collapse decides instead to levitate. Flight like that is sure to arrest the attention of ever more new residents of our city, stumbling onto a wilderness in a place they cannot explain.

Once upon a time, this was a far different place. Studded with giant Douglas fir and other climax species of evergreen and deciduous trees, forest habitat dominated the area. Then, before the turn of the 20th century, Pope & Talbot, the oldest lumber company in the Pacific Northwest, logged it. Land that was not saved by timber-baron Cyrus Walker

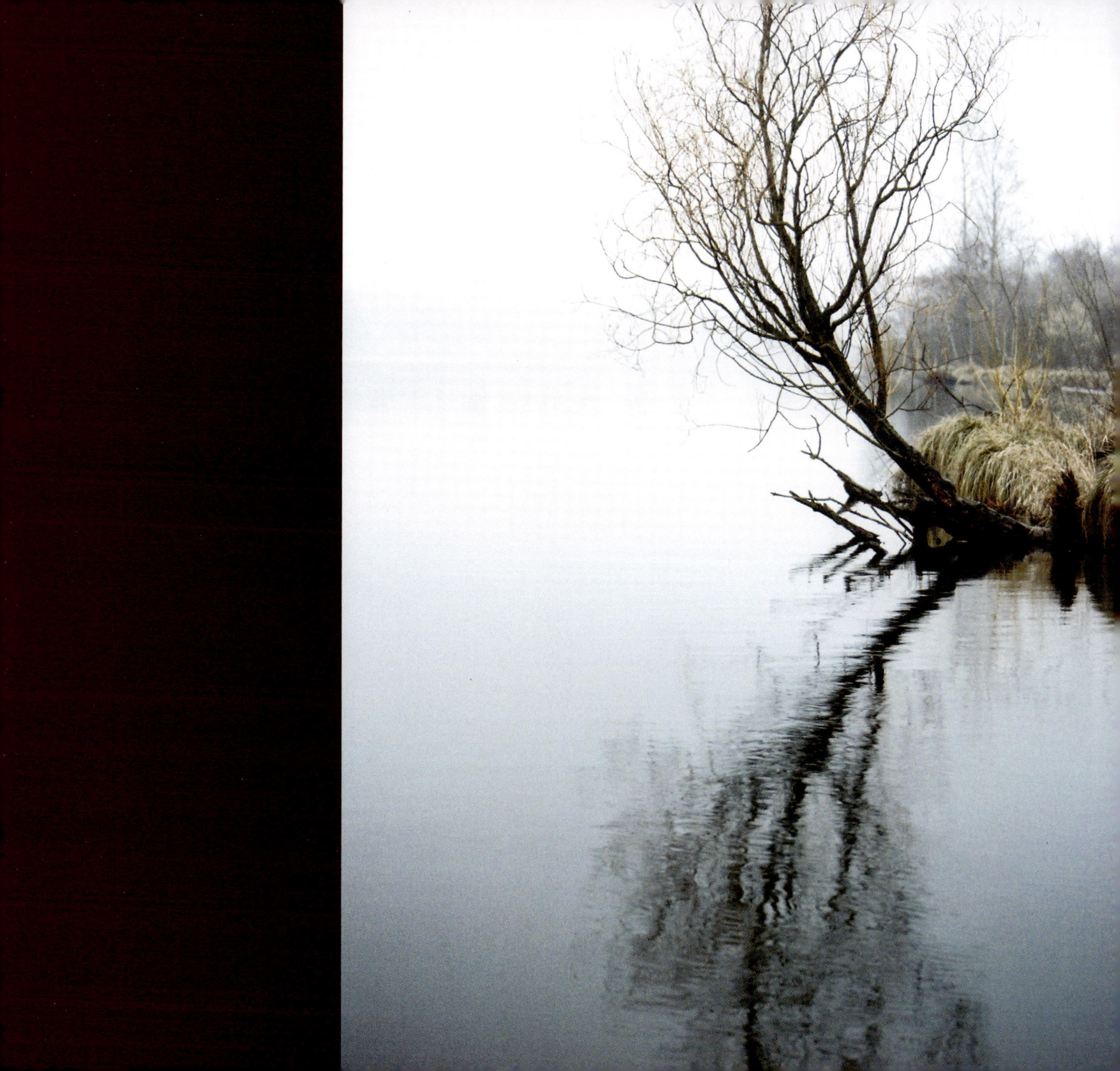

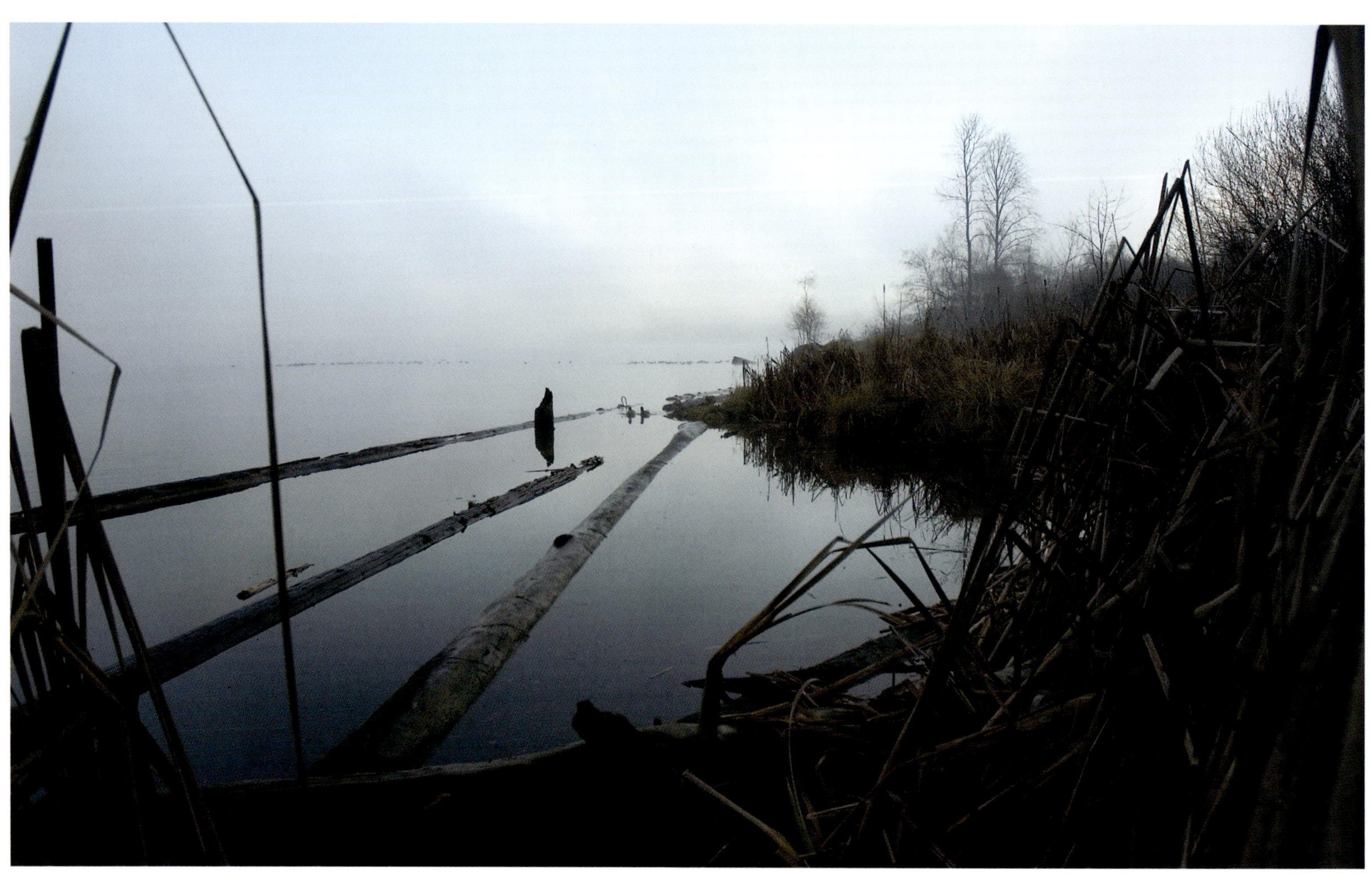

became the Washington Park Arboretum, or the adjoining neighborhoods of Madison Park, Washington Park, and Broadmoor, which were served by a trolley car system to downtown. The wetlands changed still more with the opening of the ship canal in 1917, which lowered Lake Washington's water level by nearly 11 feet. The newly exposed virgin lake-bottom was soon consumed by water lilies, reeds, cattails, and willows. These in turn provided habitat for birds, insects, and the occasional mammal.

Today, the peace and artistry of the place is profound—quiet, yet teeming with life, an environment that is home to many and succor to those of us just passing through. It inspires artists and bids the curious to explore.

After years of experiencing the many surprises, wonders, and delights of the wetlands, we have come to realize that most of those who live here have no idea that all of this goes on. Our friends stare in disbelief at our stories, as if we were describing some distant travels rather than a casual stroll or paddle in the middle of our city. We have also come to realize that many Seattleites are proud of these mysterious wetlands, a wonderful, wild secret that we see as proof of our city's greatness.

All great cities have a soul, and Seattle's arises from a deep entanglement with the wild. We are surrounded by slumbering volcanoes, pierced through by massive, unexpected runs of salmon. Eagles choose our trees to raise their young. Coyotes still howl at night. And on the water's edge, pinned between a freeway and quiet, orderly neighborhoods, there exists a place with more wildness, beauty, and surprise than could be imagined.

Explore this book. We hope that, to your surprise, you discover the wild within.

— *Michael and Lisa Anderson*

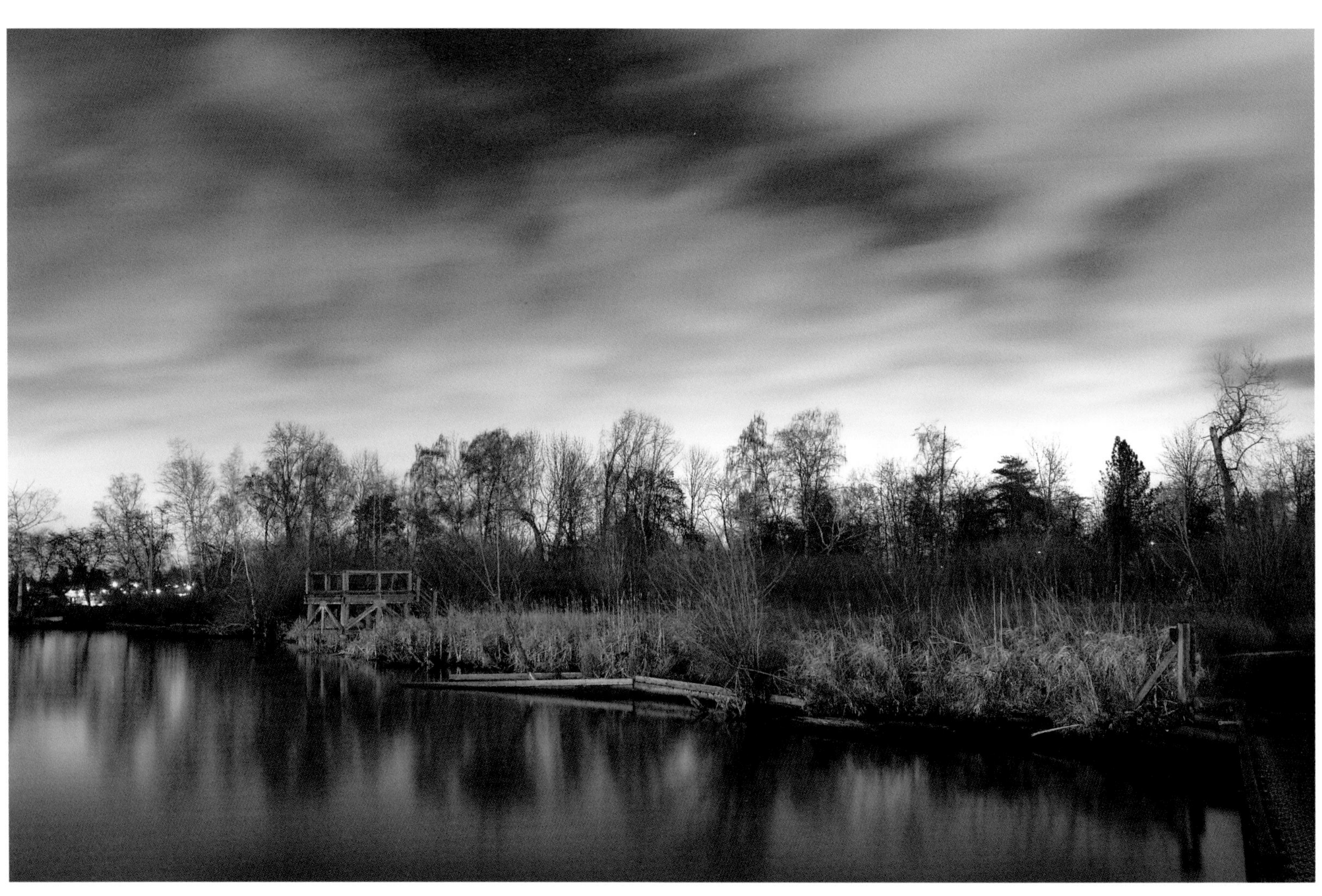

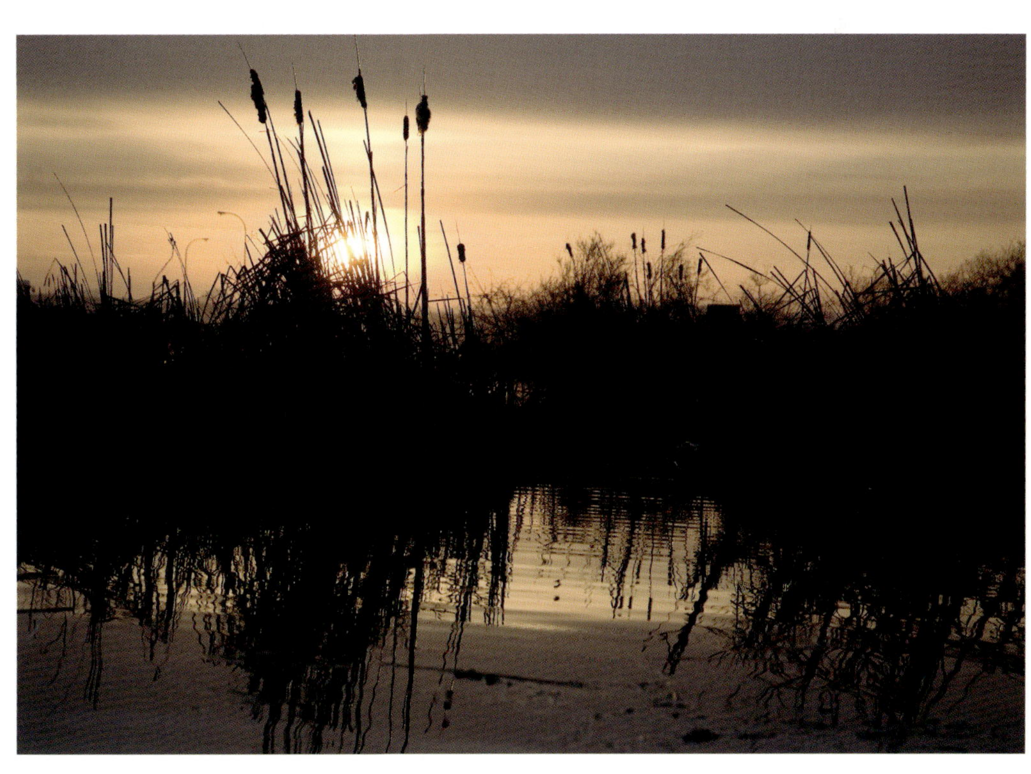

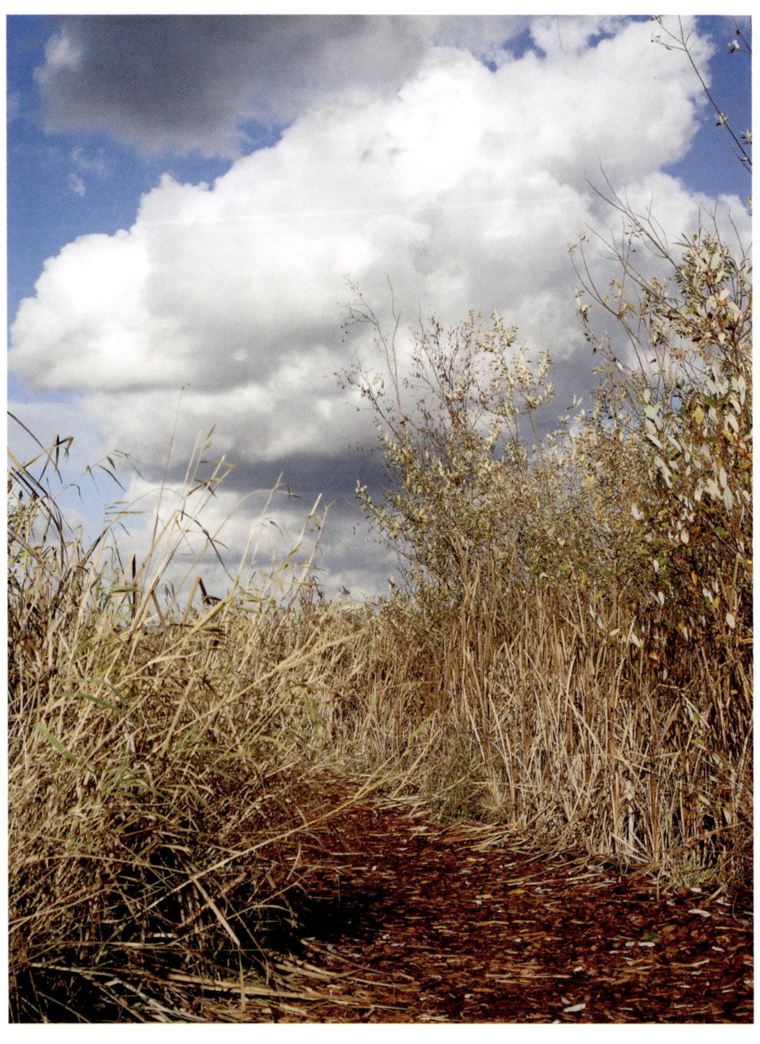

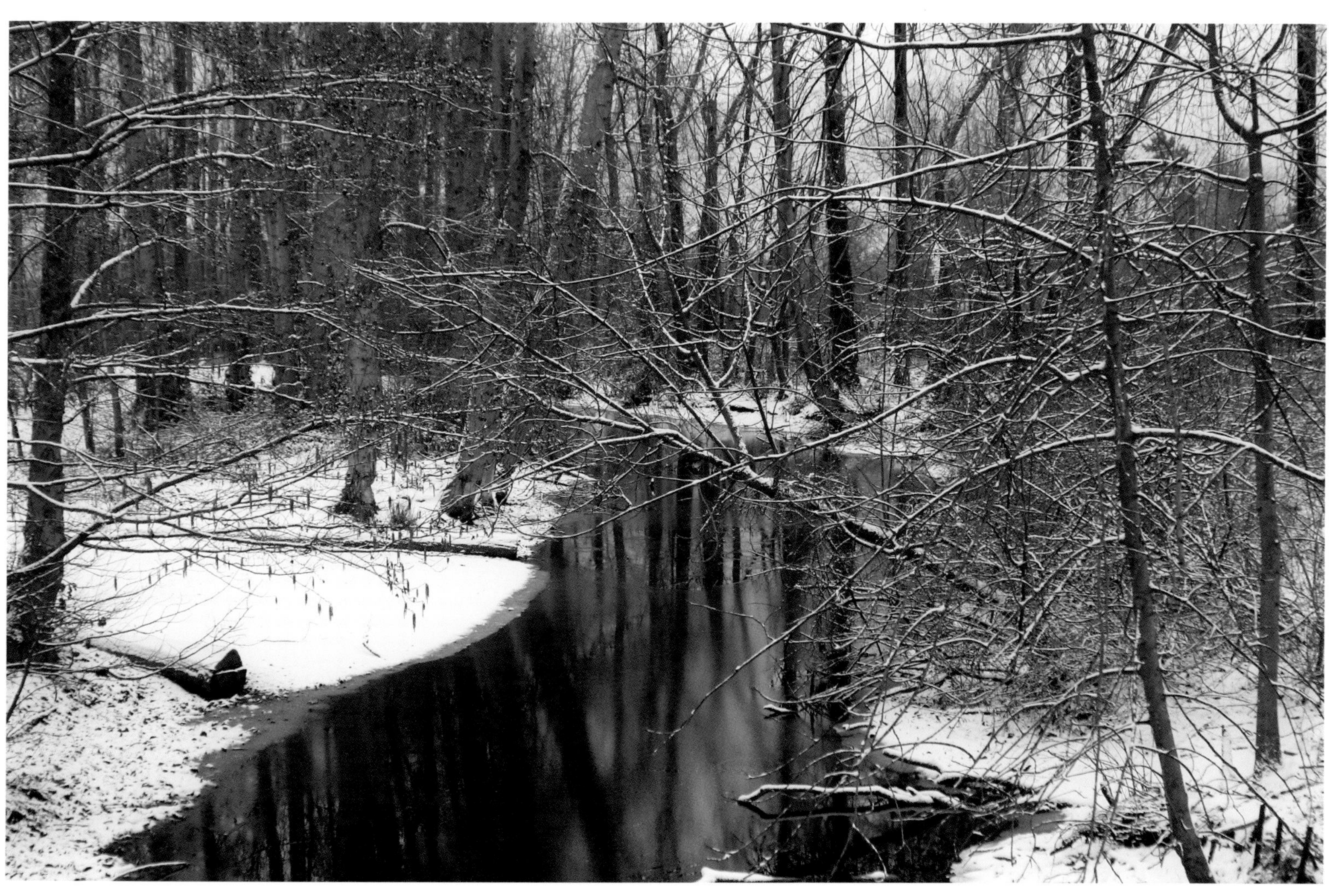

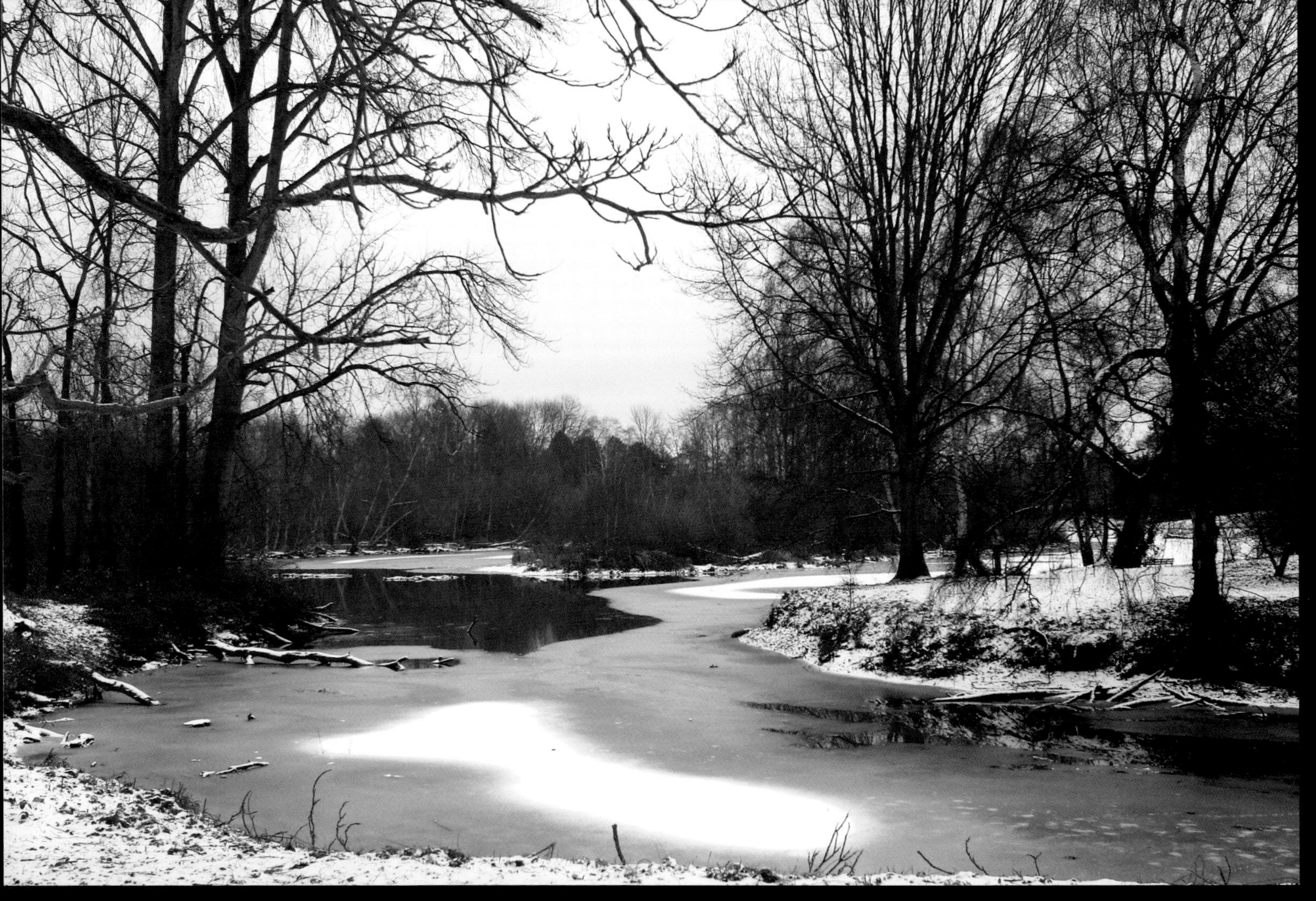

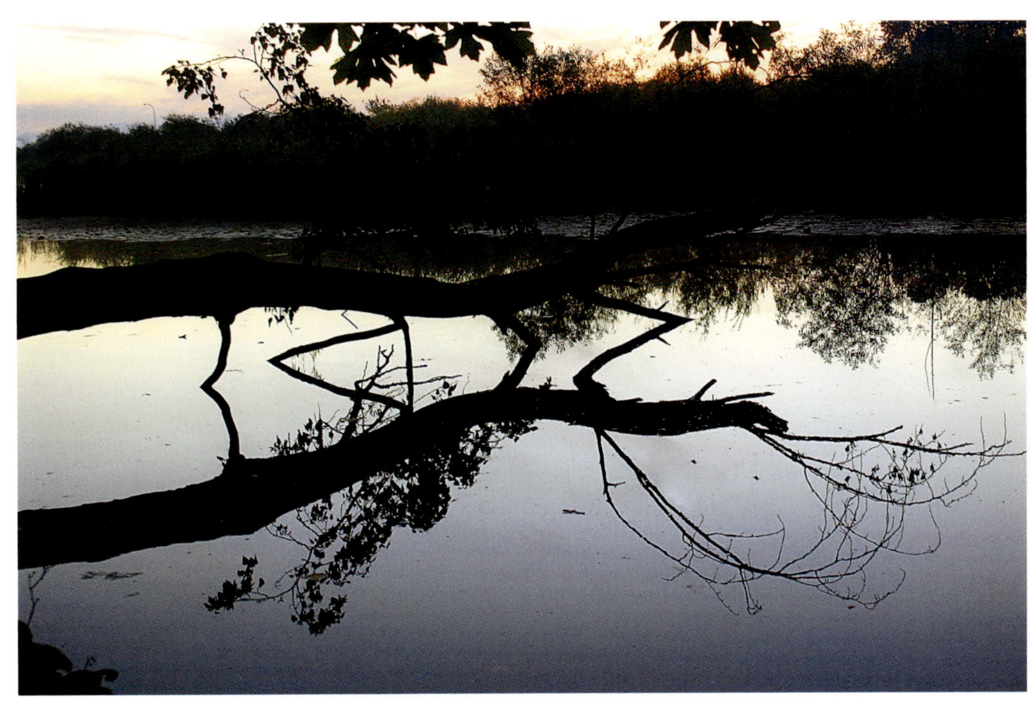

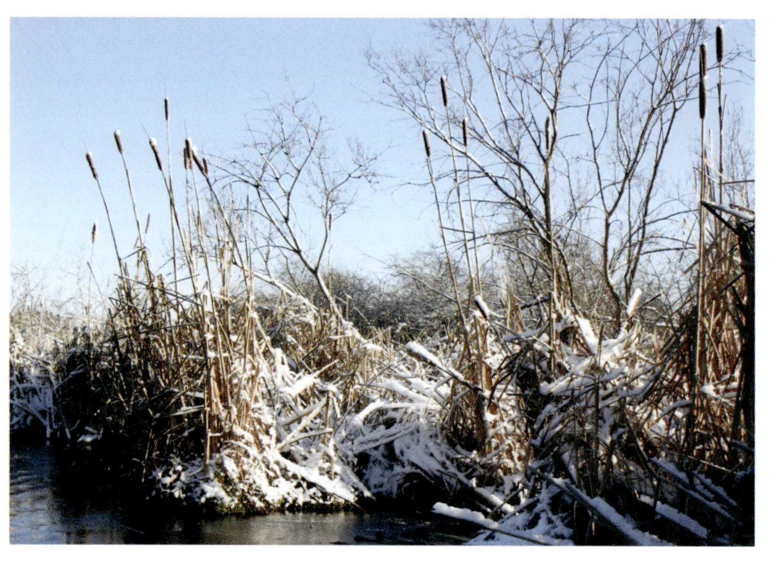

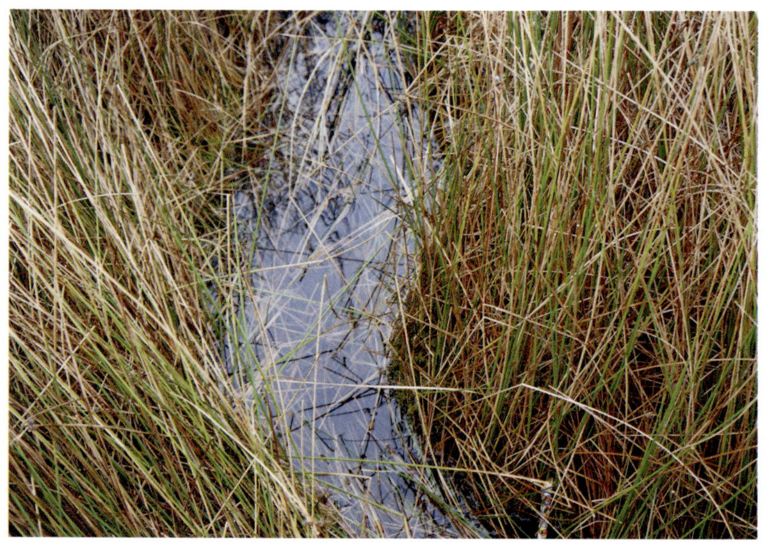

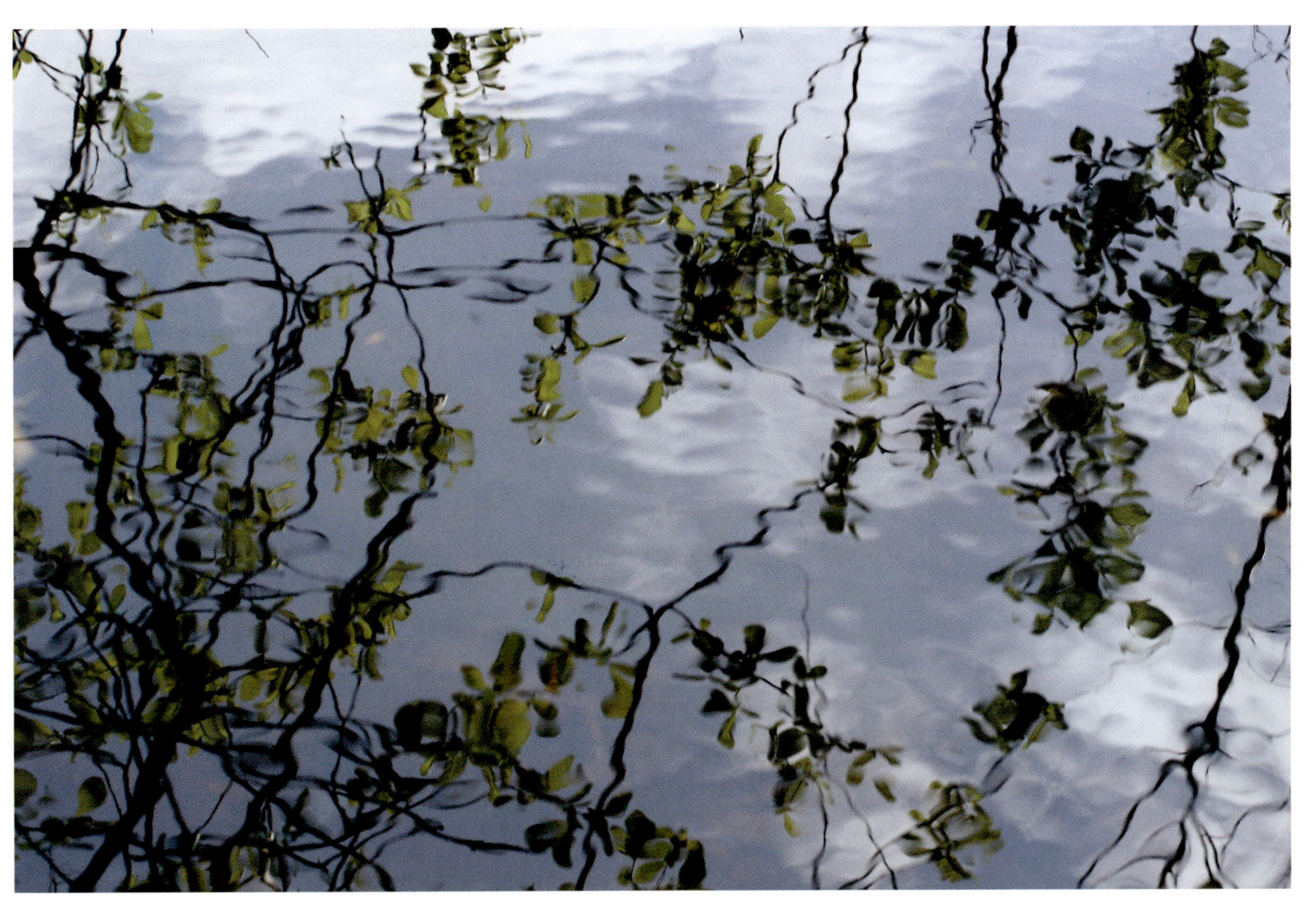

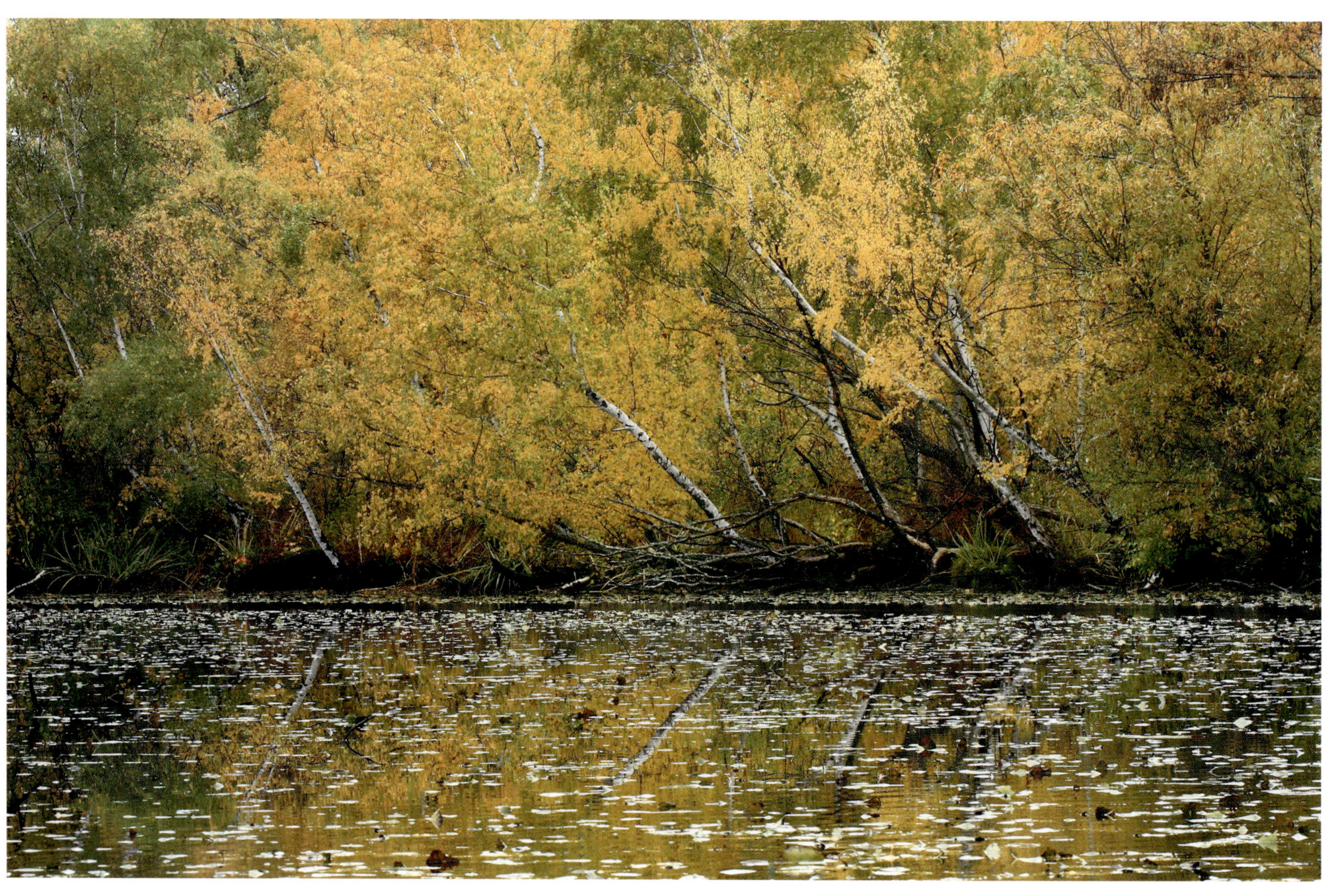

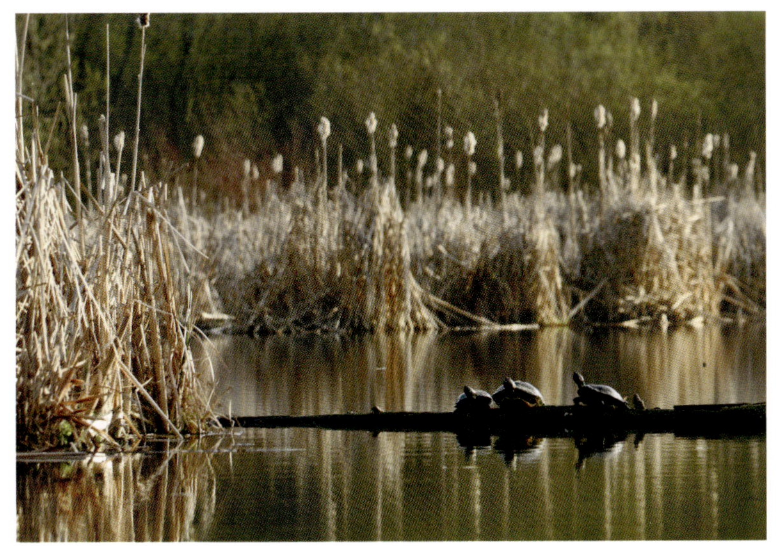

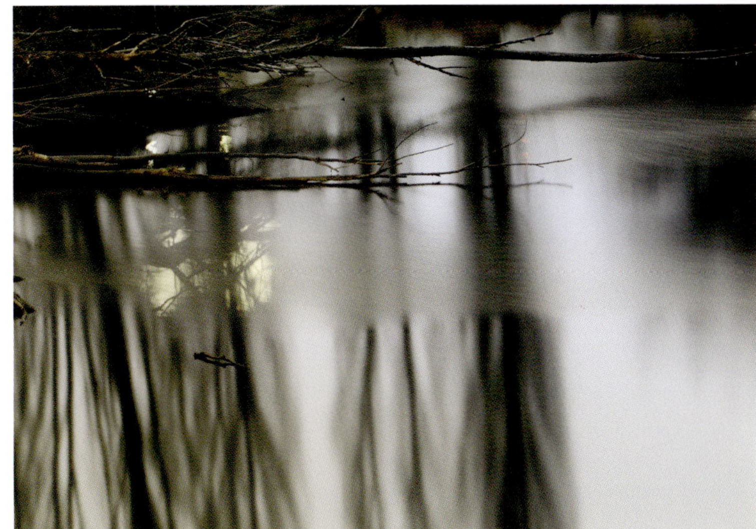

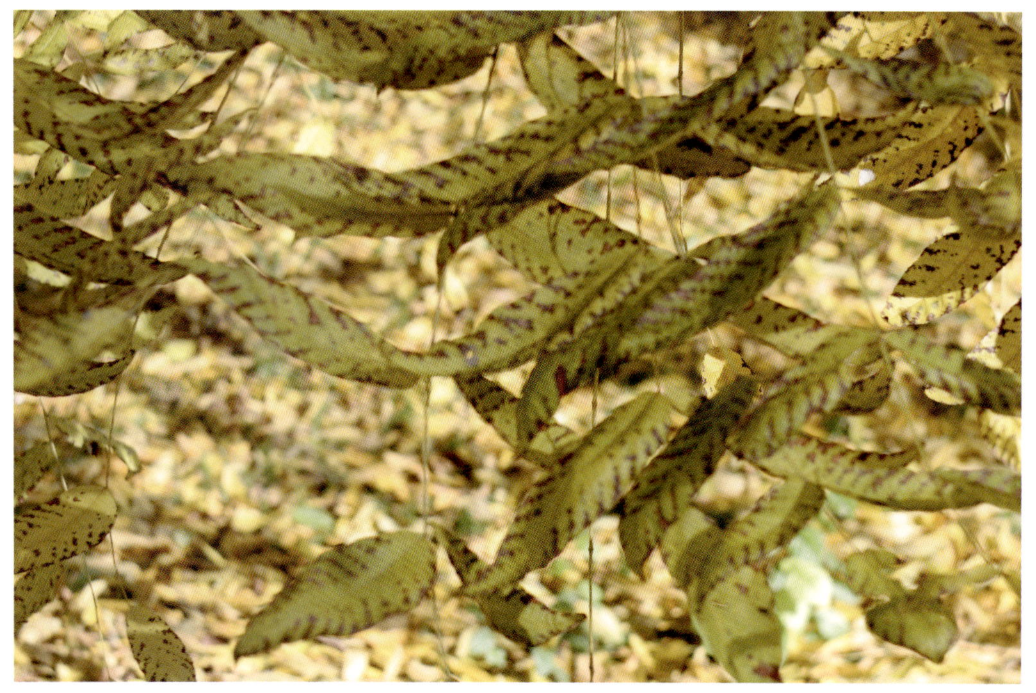

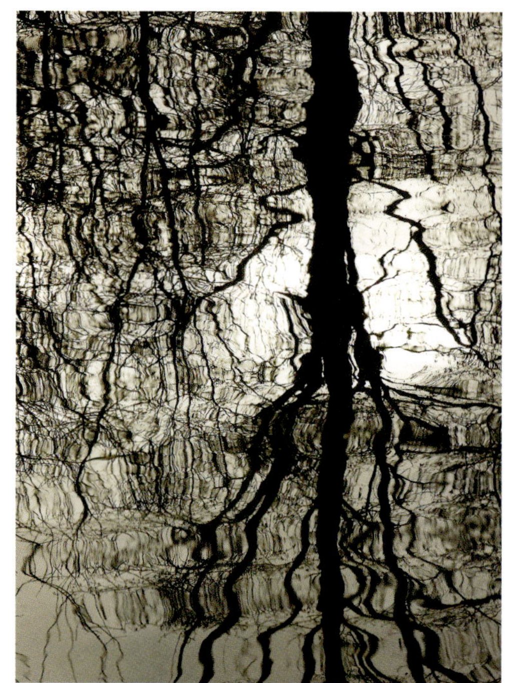

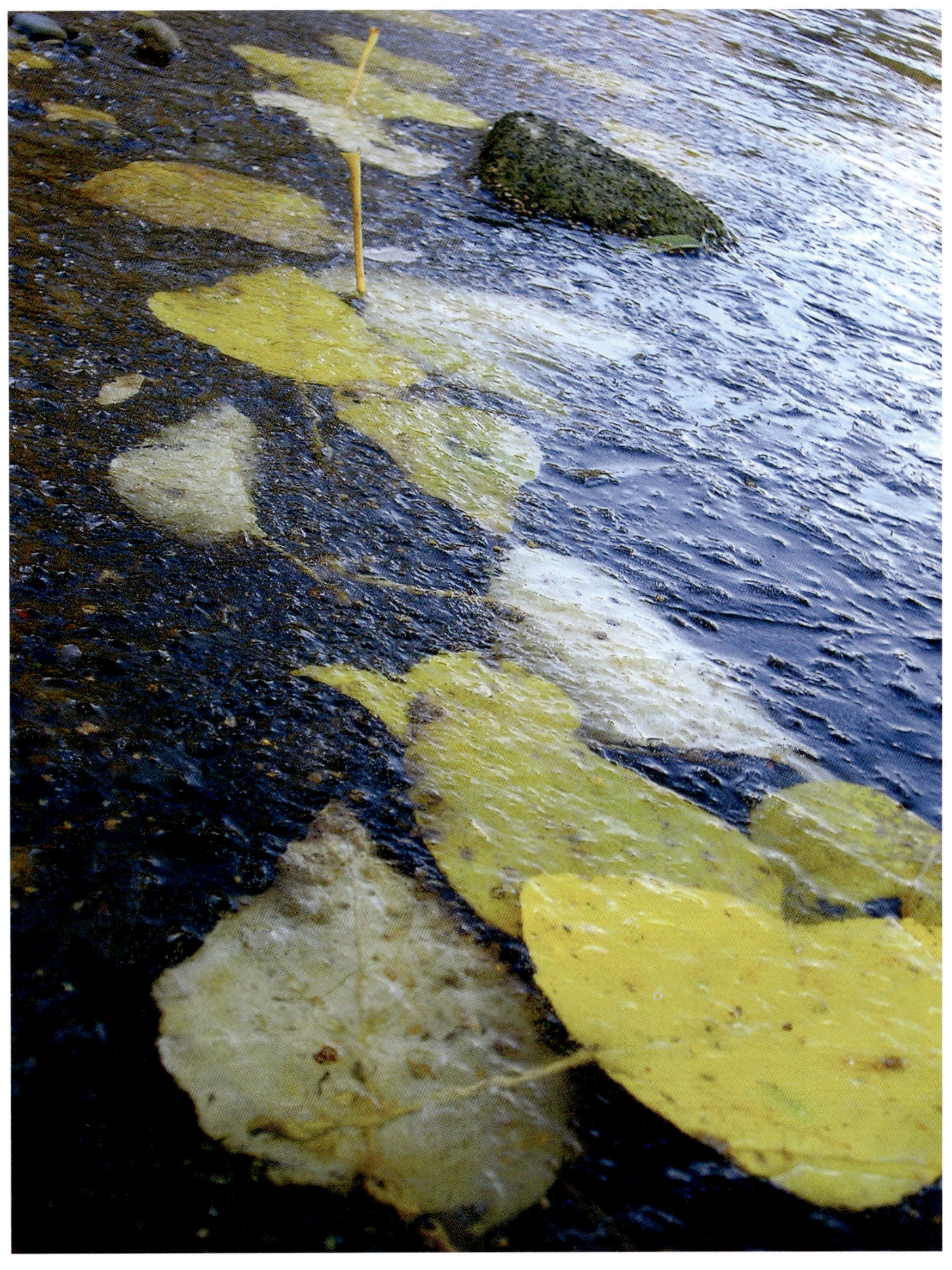

I live at the water's edge, and I've always lived close to water. When I was a student at the University of Washington, I lived on a houseboat in Mallard Cove tethered to the east shore of Lake Union, not far from the Arboretum's wetlands. That was before the freeway, and it was quiet then.

The connections between glass and water are unbelievable to me, so organic, so visual. Instead of glass I once created an installation made of block ice, then watched it melt unevenly next to a wall in Jerusalem under the Middle Eastern sun. It created a lasting memory.

A few years ago I placed an installation in the enclosed waters of the Washington Park Arboretum wetlands. I had created large blue crystal shapes for a garden, but they never looked quite right to me. I thought they might look good in water, so we took them to the Arboretum and set them along the shoreline, and the juxtaposition between the glass and the natural elements was striking. The crystals that never looked quite right to me in a garden really looked good reflected in the dark water, surrounded by sticks, leaves, and water lilies.

I have created herons, hornets, red reeds, yellow reeds, and lilies of glass, all things you might expect to find in the wetlands, and the works have been placed in and around water. They seemed to belong there.

I want my glass to appear as if it came from nature. Somebody who found a piece of my glass along the shoreline or among a tangle of trees might think it belonged there. That would be quite satisfying.

— *Dale Chihuly*

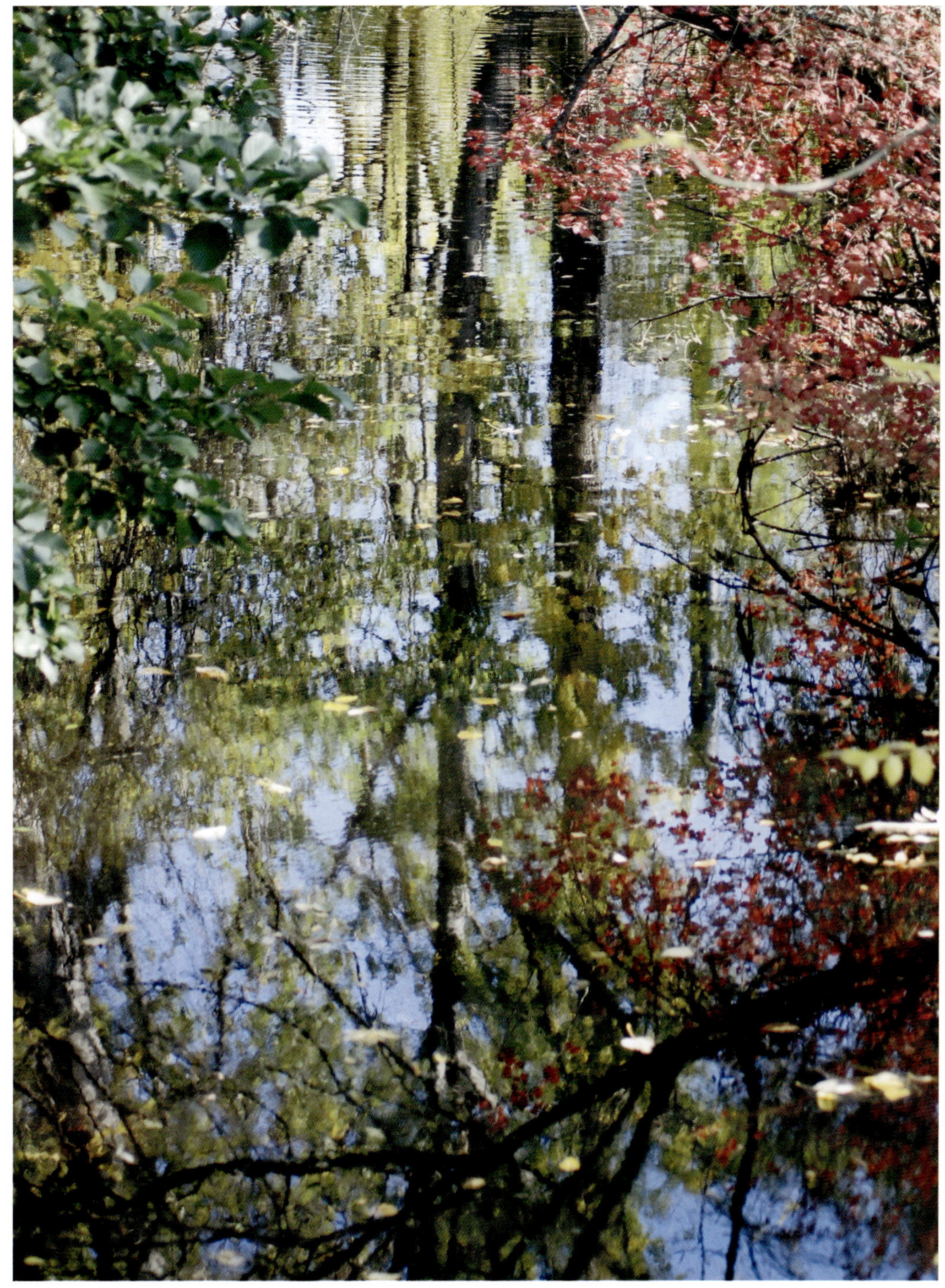

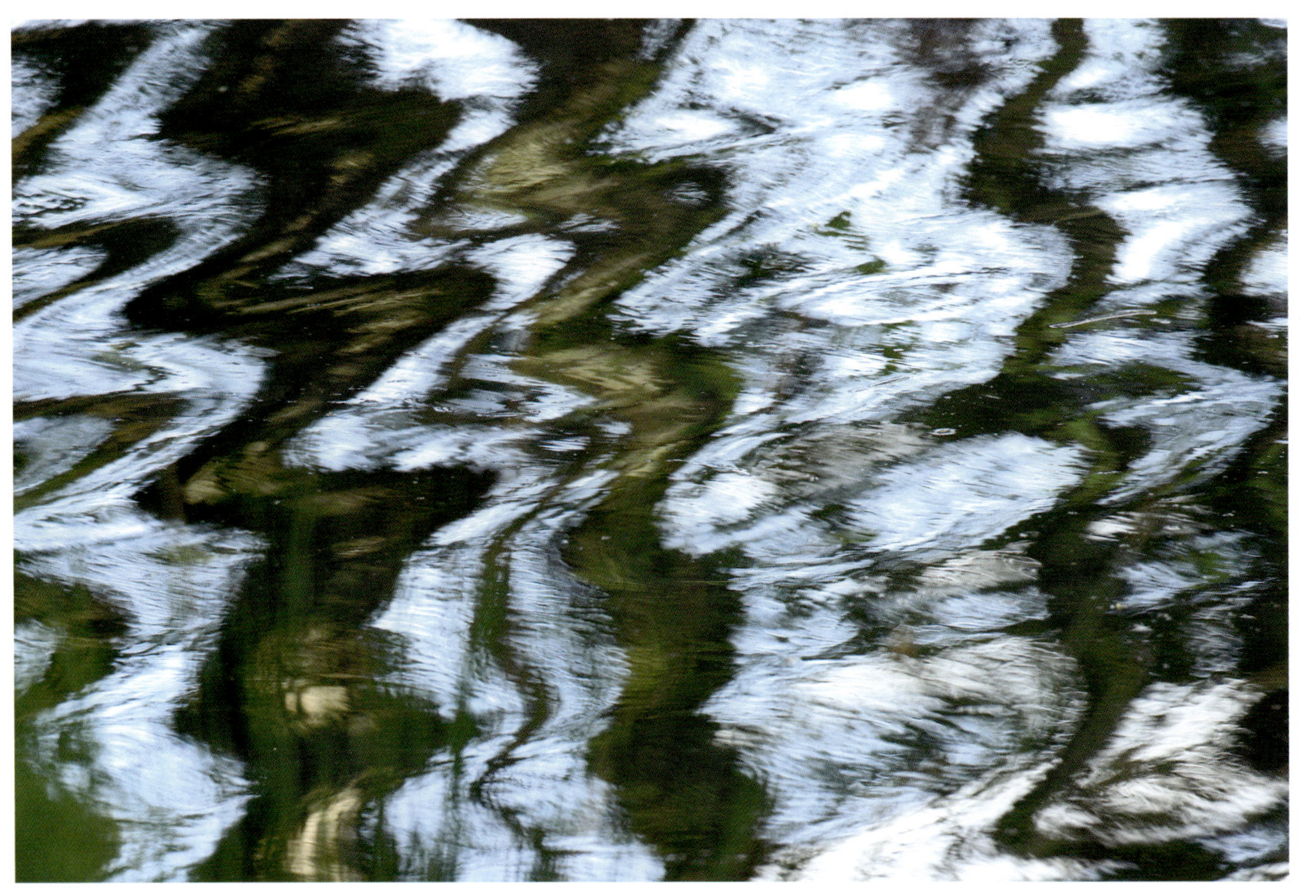

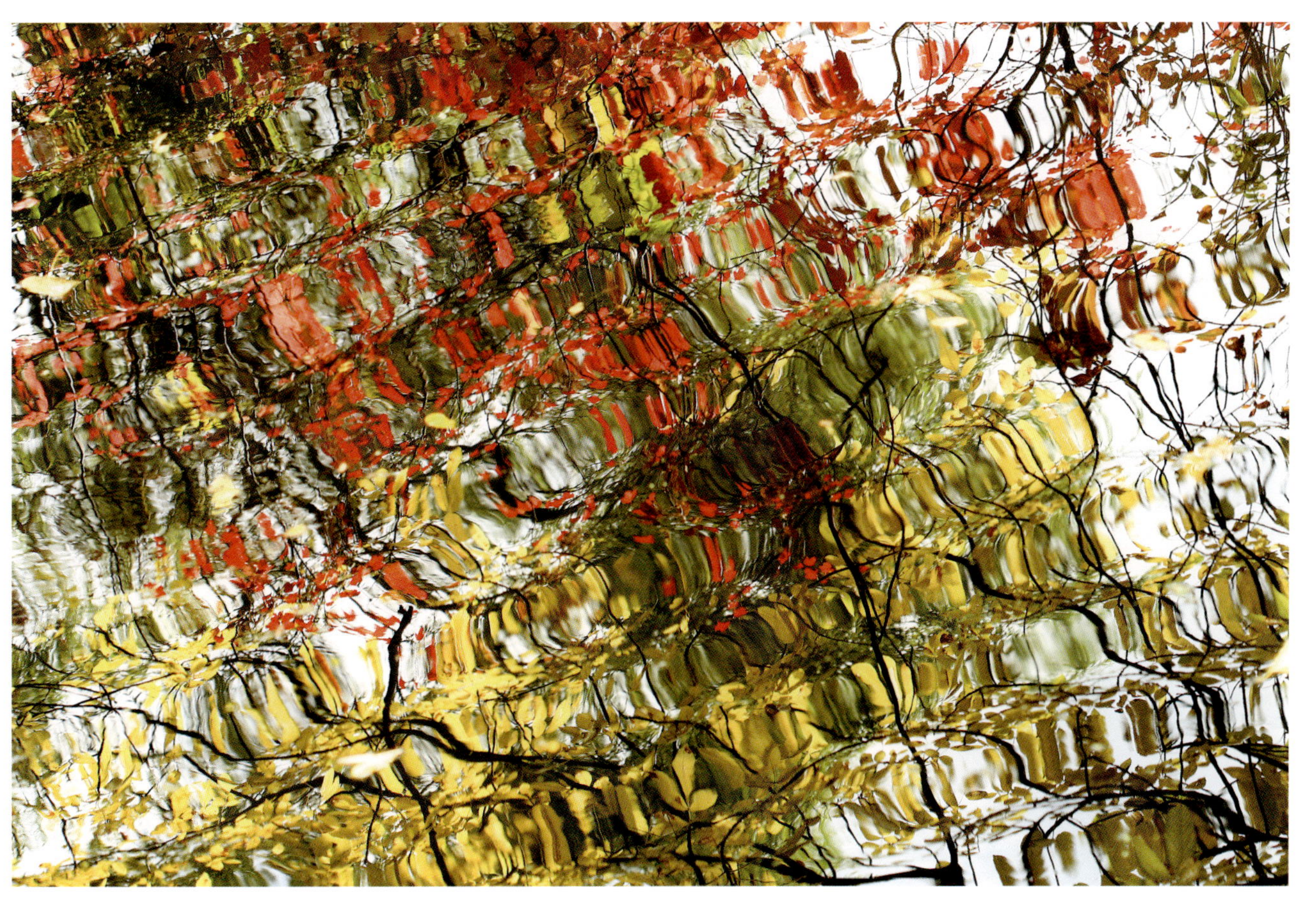

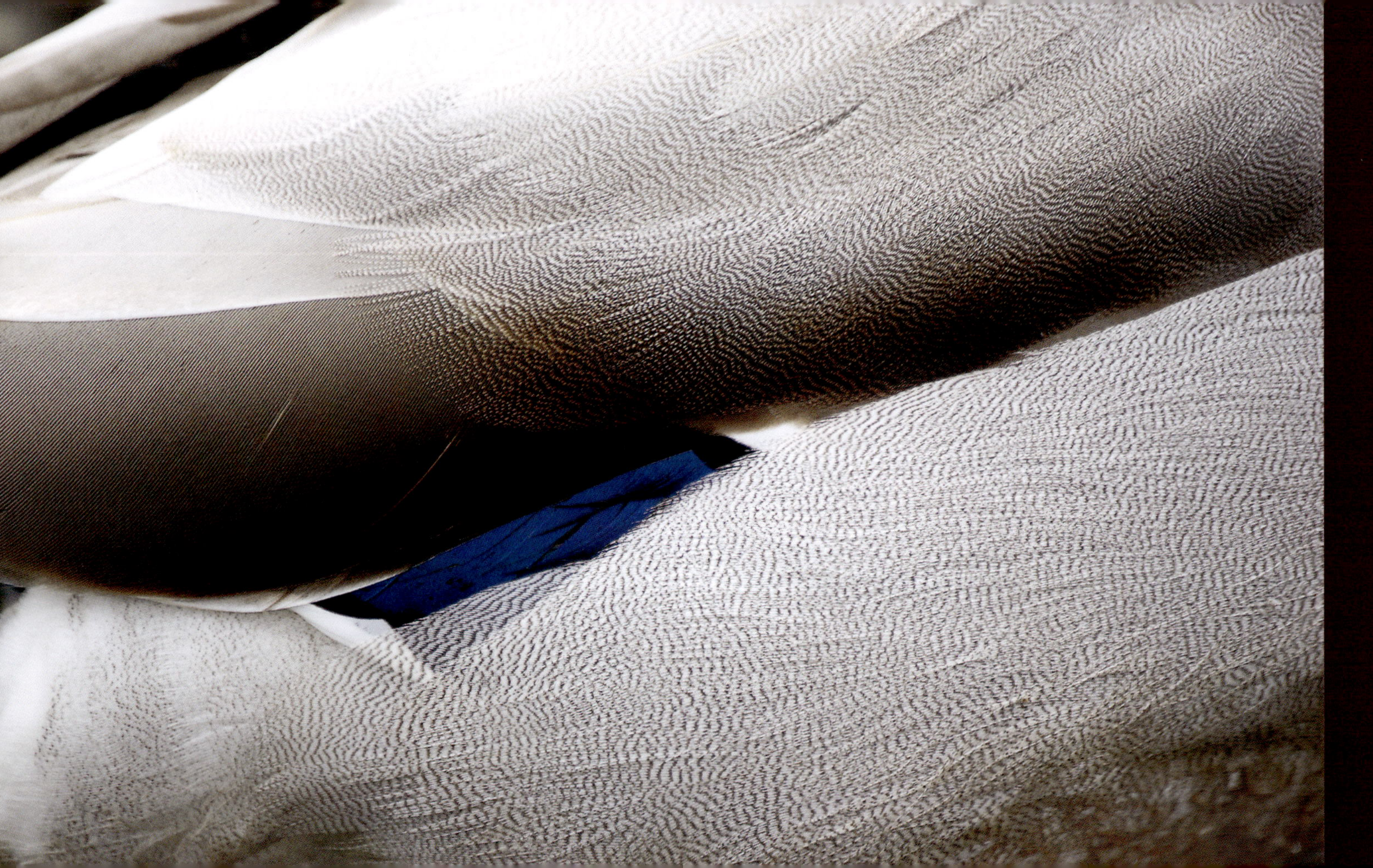

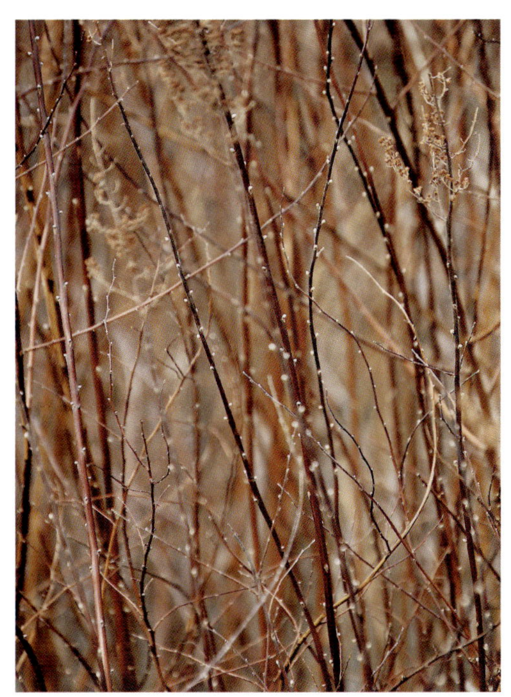

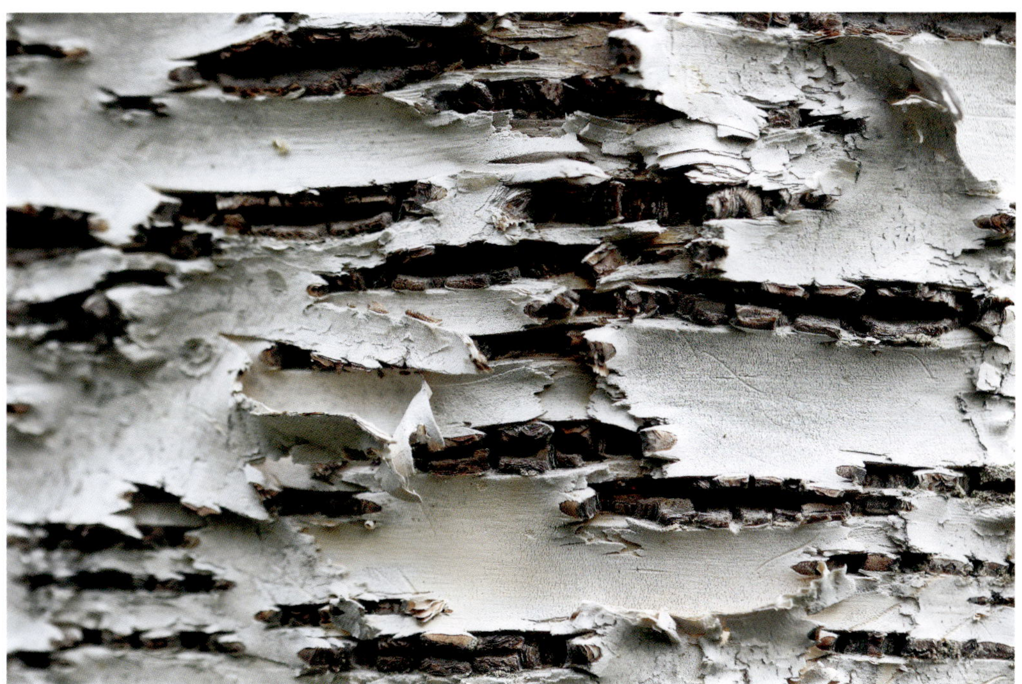

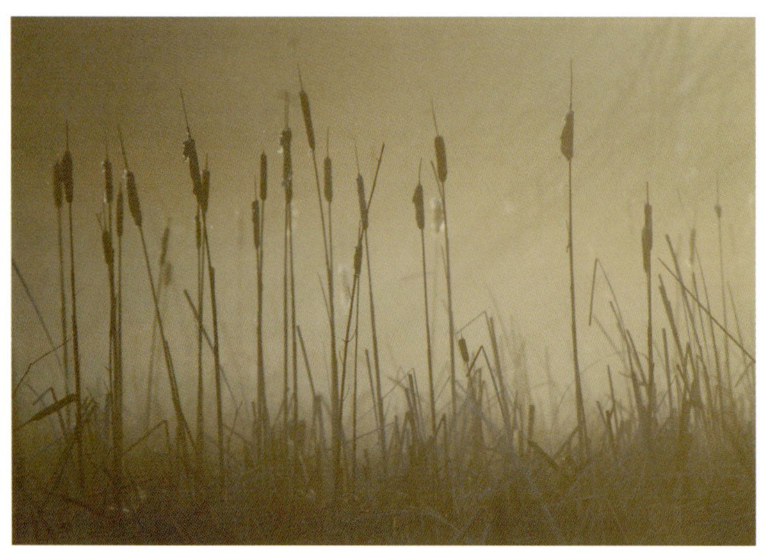

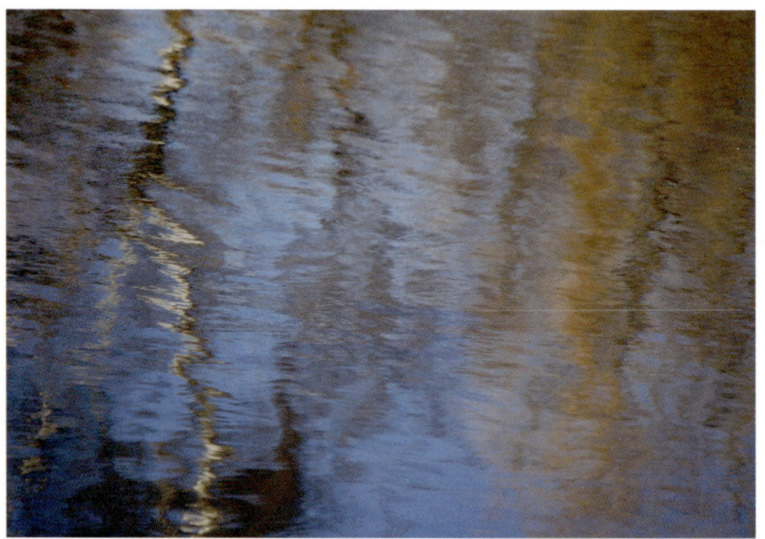

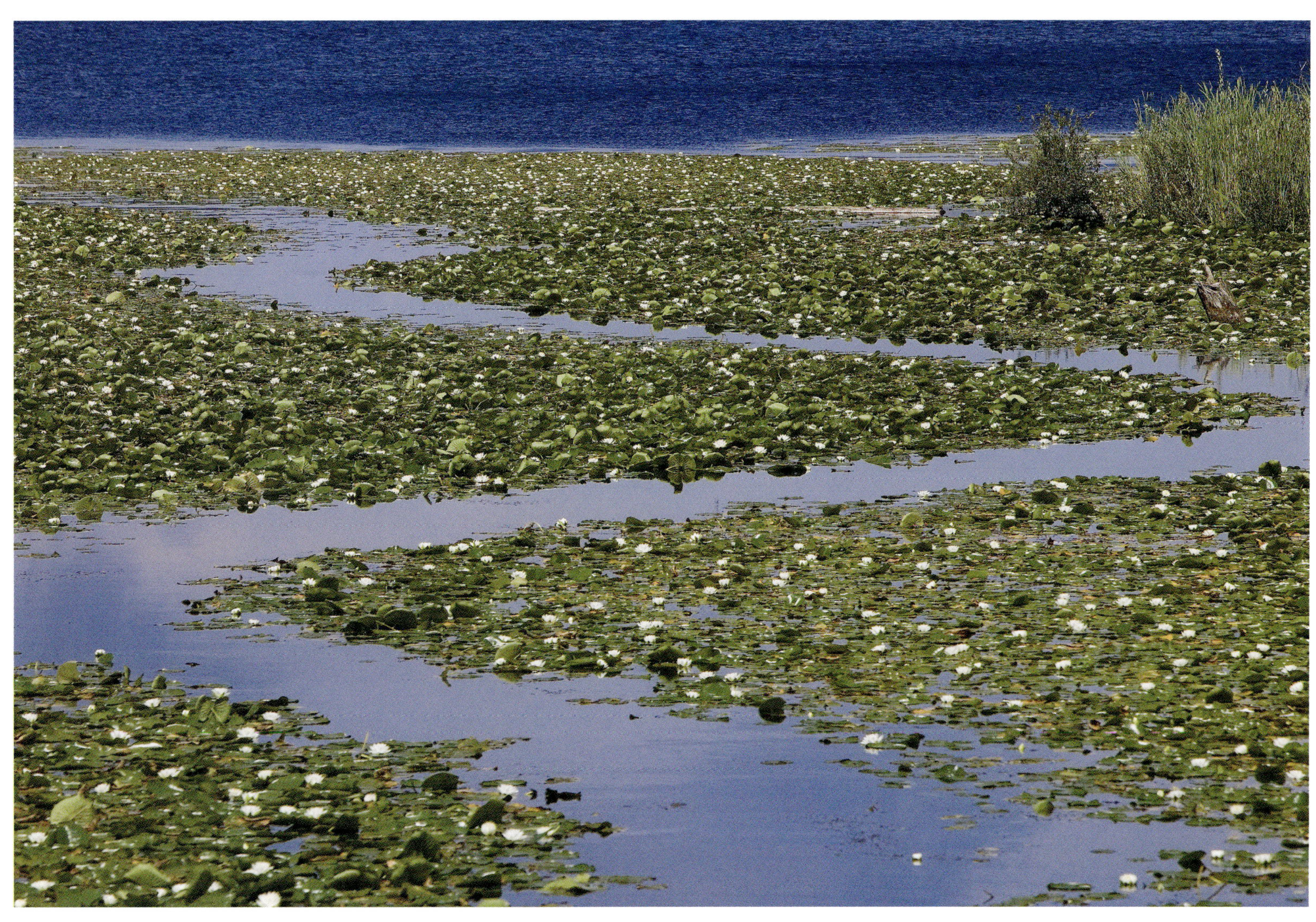

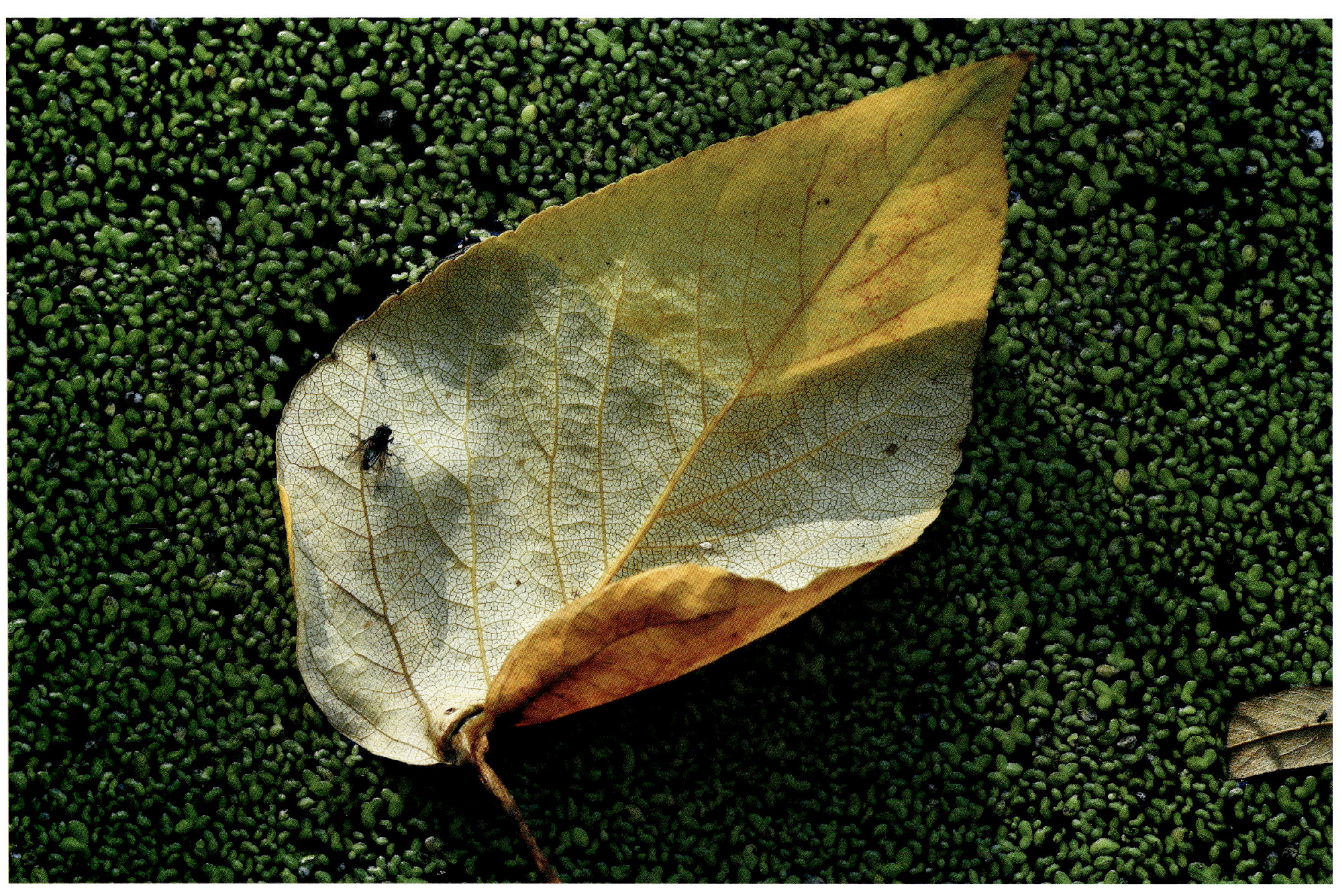

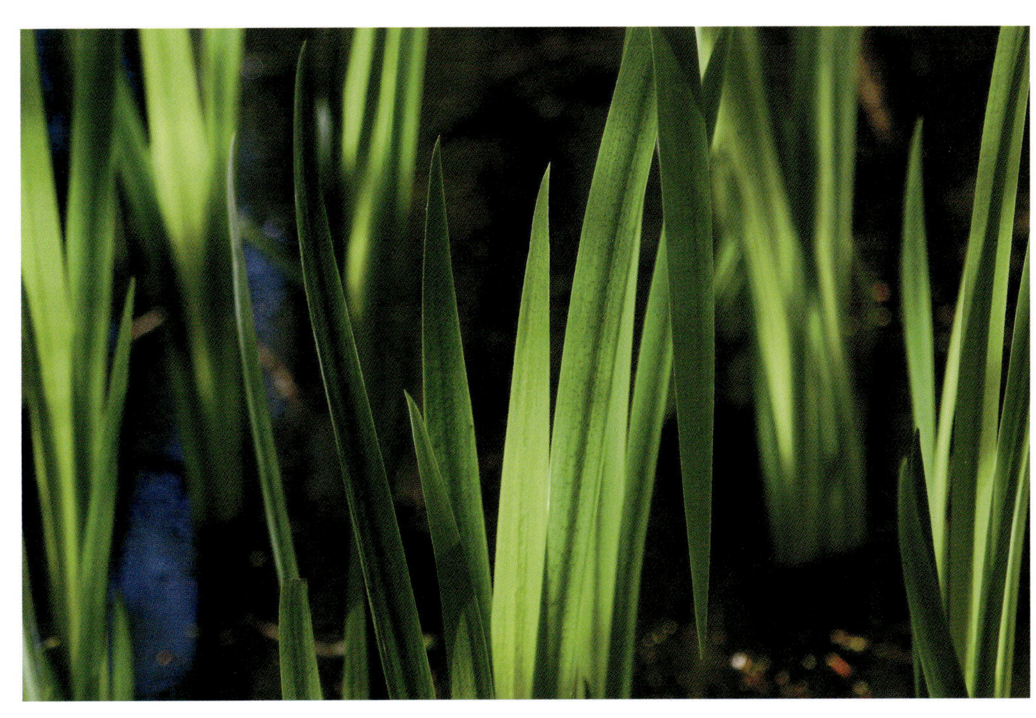

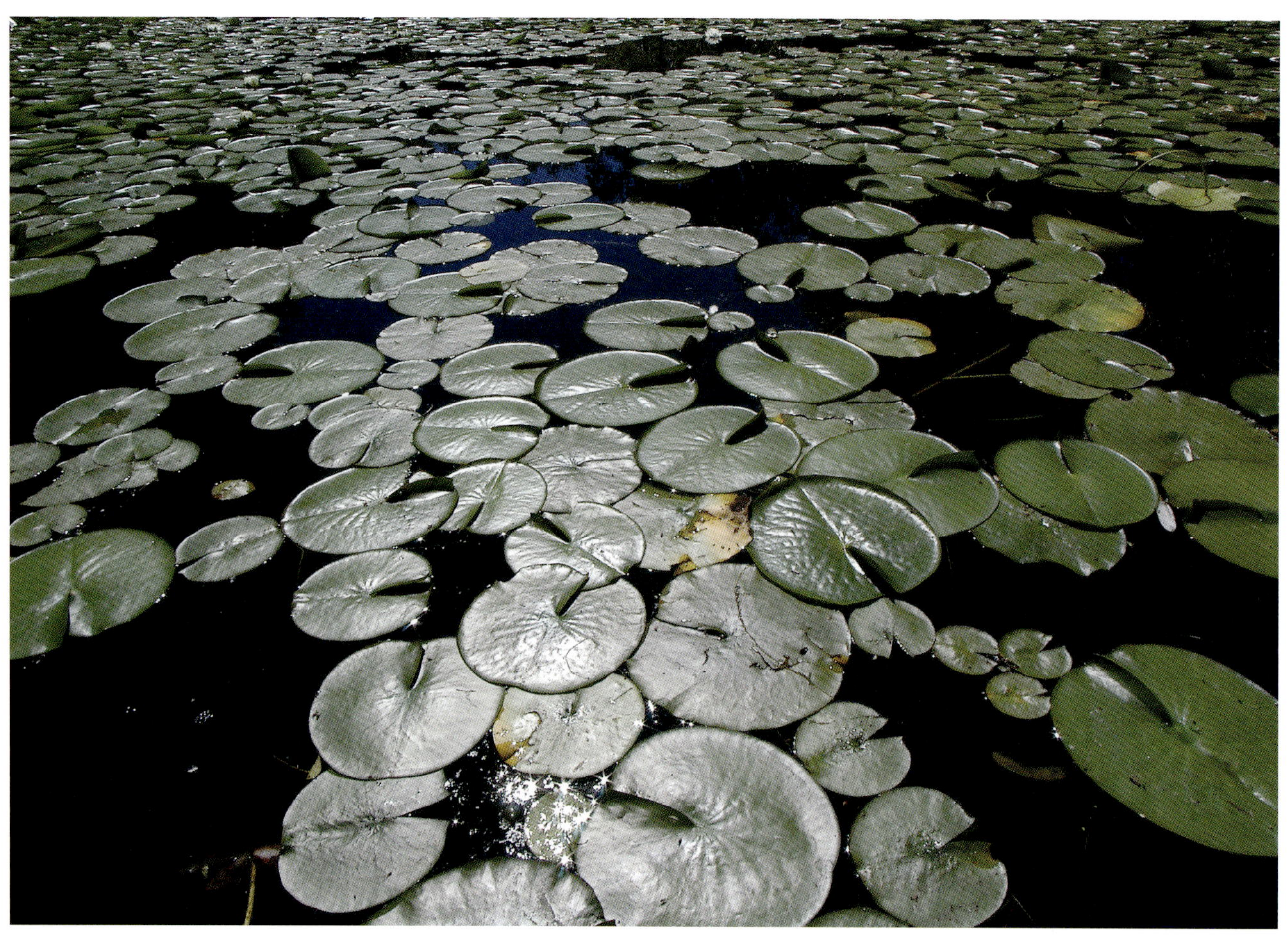

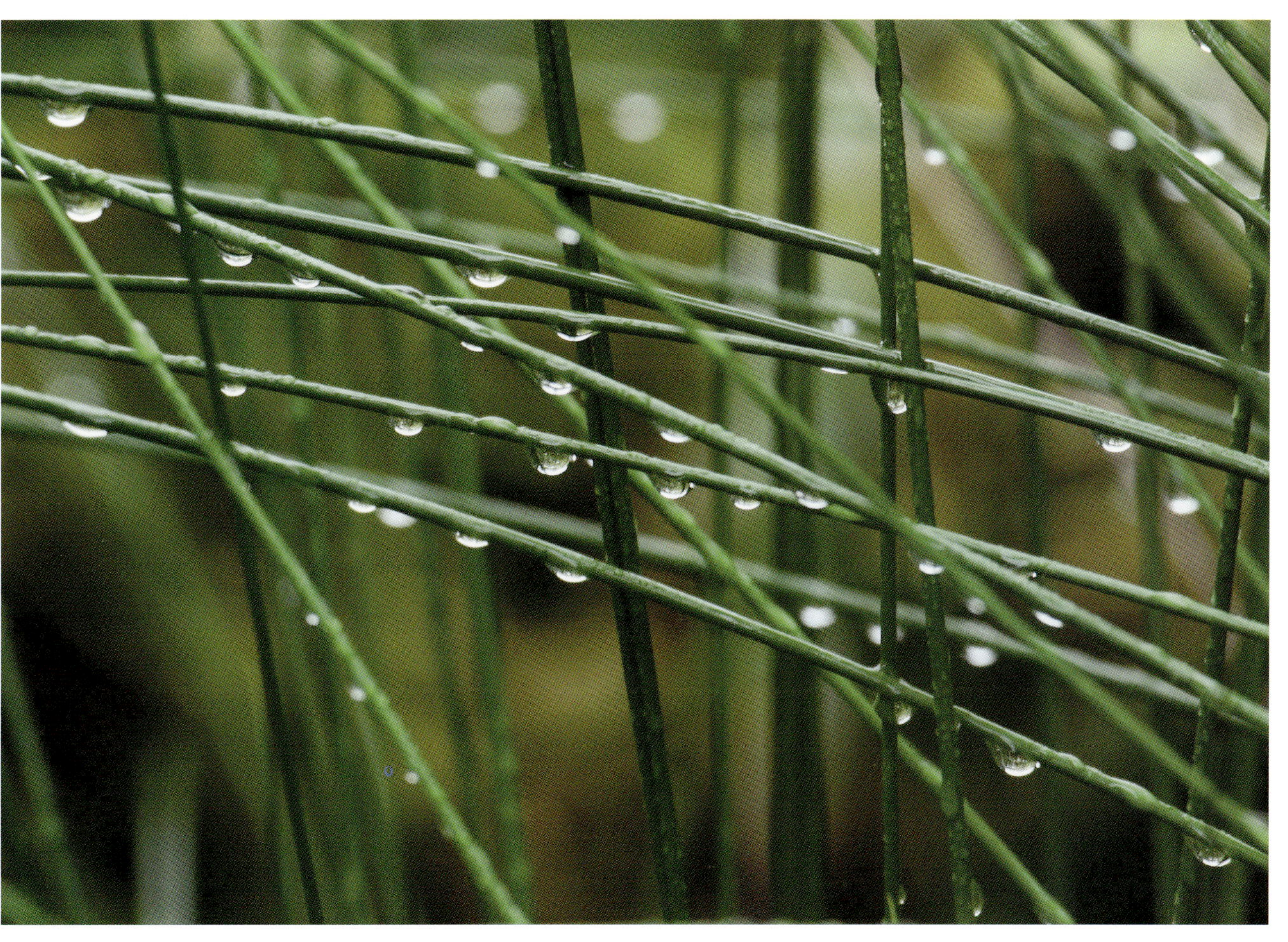

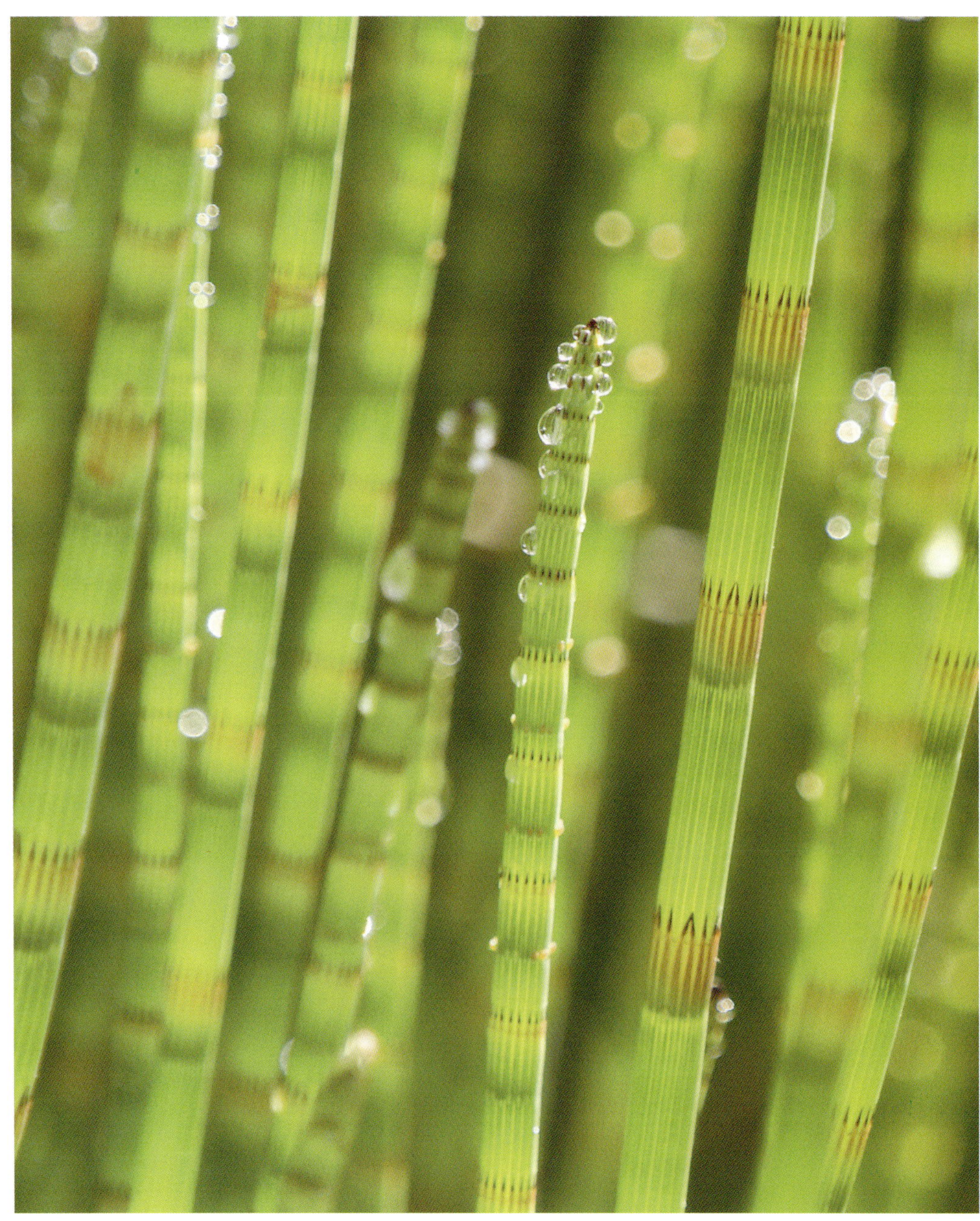

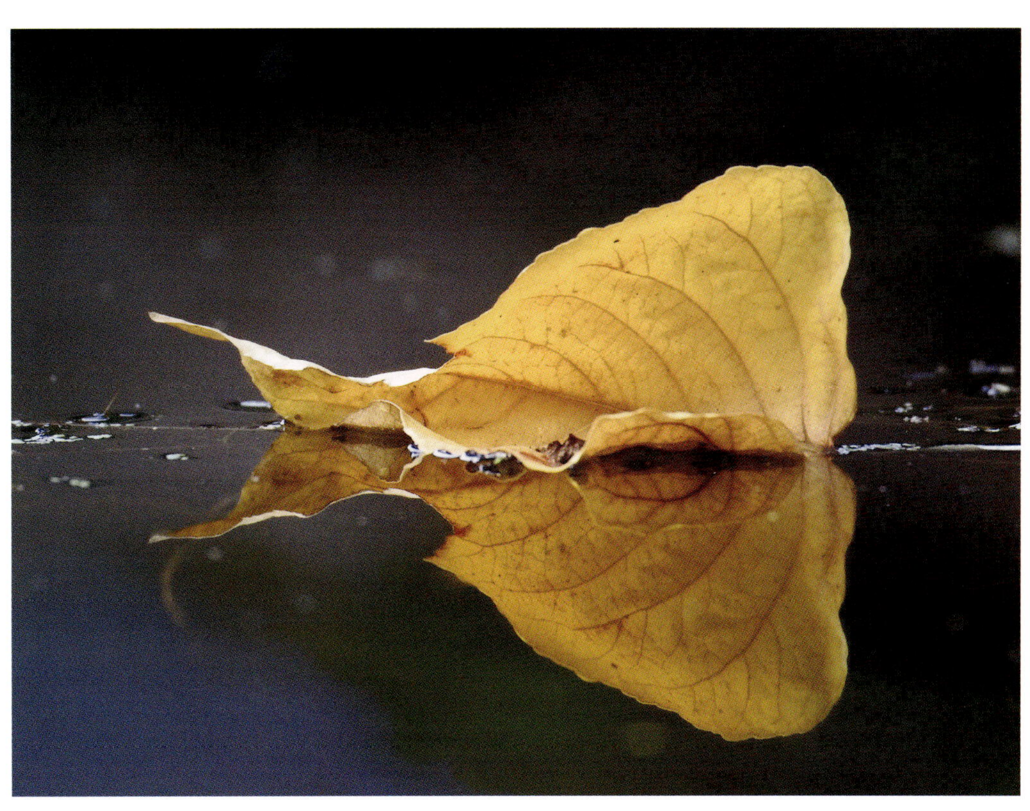

Without the touchstone of a pure earth, how do we know what we are doing to this planet and to the natural bounties that we all depend upon?

Disturbed by the ever-increasing wave of species extinctions, Aldo Leopold used the analogy of the watchmaker and wrote in *A Sand County Almanac* that the first law of intelligent tinkering is to preserve all of the pieces.

With the majority of the world's people living in urban centers, these wisdoms could easily be lost, resulting in a continuing deterioration of our planet's environmental health.

How does this relate to Seattle's Arboretum wetlands (or New York's Central Park or San Francisco's Golden Gate Park)? The Arboretum wetlands are an oasis in the sea of urban development. They give us a connection to nature and allow us to appreciate and understand the natural world, which provides us with all that we need: food, water, shelter, medicines, spirituality.

How can the hundreds of thousands of visitors who drive, run, and walk through the Arboretum not be awakened by her natural beauty? The Arboretum forests and wetlands cleanse us. Seasons, blossoms, ducks, herons, bald eagles, songbirds, pollinating insects, smells of forest and understory connect us to life and allow us to think about more than the immediate issues that capture so much of our mind space.

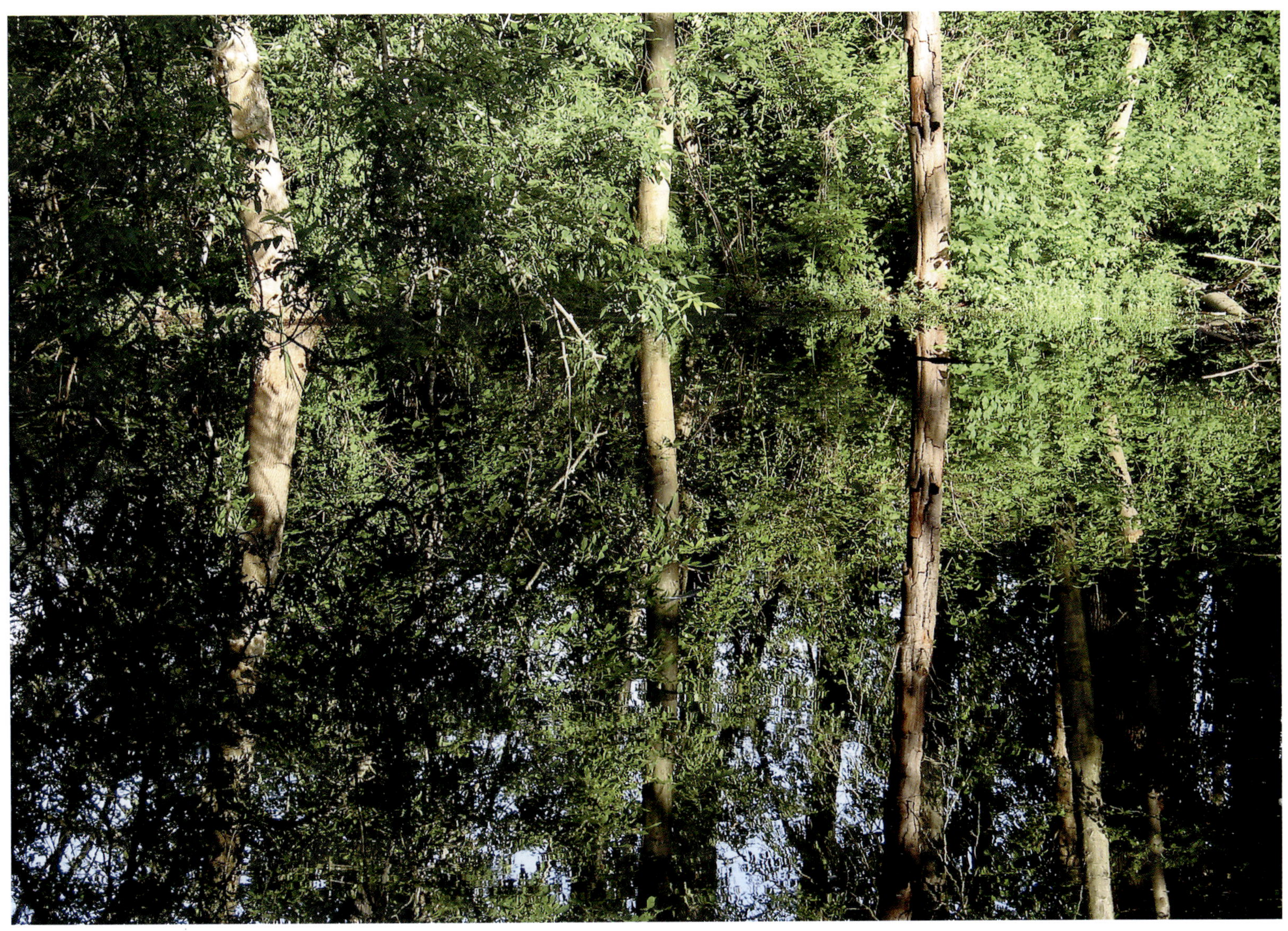

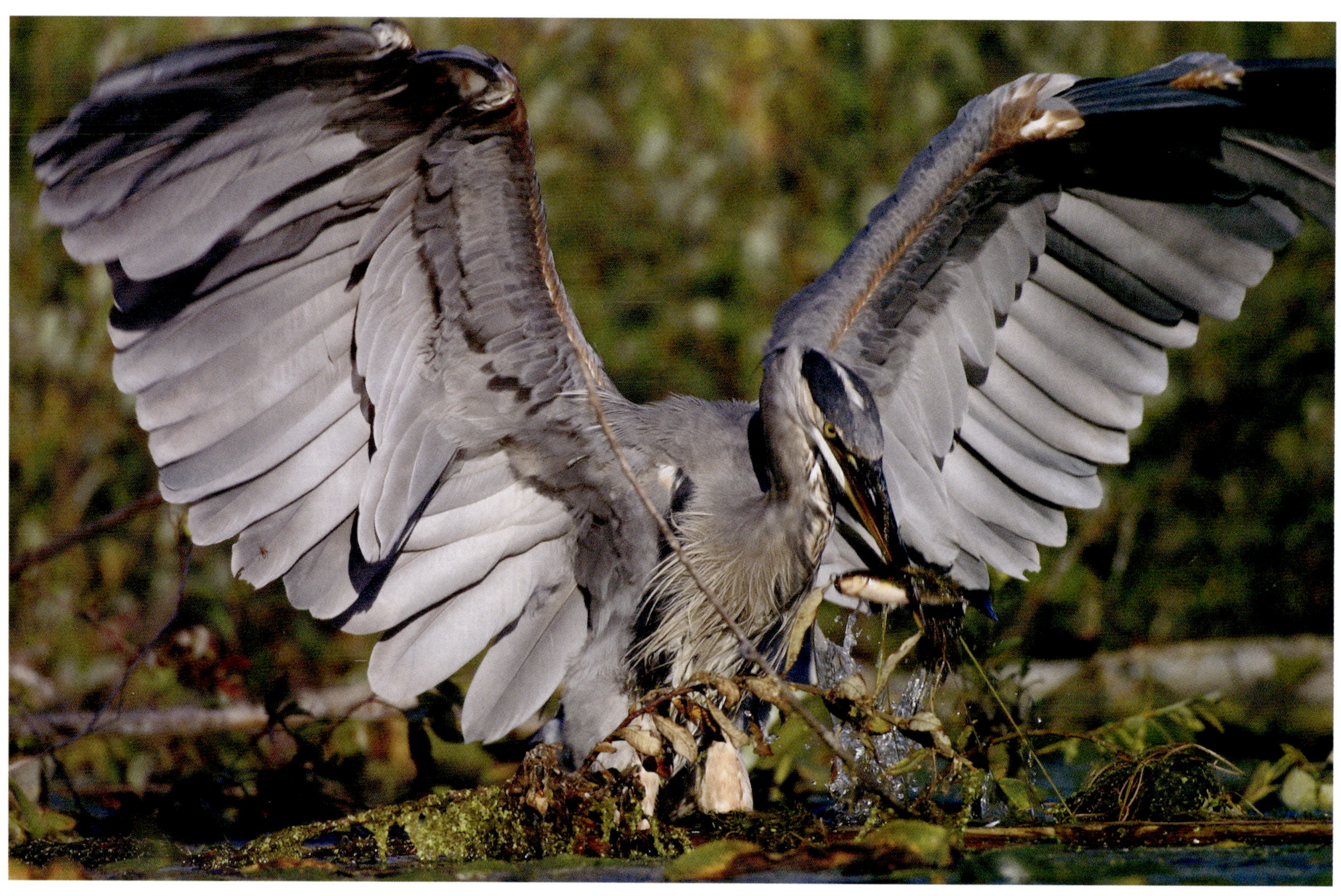

We will preserve this earth, our common ground, if we awaken to her gifts. This is the gift of the Arboretum. This is the gift that our ancestors, the wise people who saved these wetlands, bestowed upon us. This is the gift that we, if we preserve the health of this earth, will give to our children.

It is not enough to preserve special places. We must deepen our understanding of our dependence upon the earth for survival. The stark truth is that how we and the next few generations treat nature will determine our place in history. Our moments on the earth are but brief. What will we leave our descendants? When we invest in their education about nature and our dependence upon her, we will spawn the global conservation ethic that will allow this one place in our universe where we live to survive.

In a basic way, then, the Arboretum is our salvation. It is the route by which the urban population will understand that the natural world is the common ground we all share.

— Peter Seligmann

Co-Founder, Chair, and CEO, Conservation International

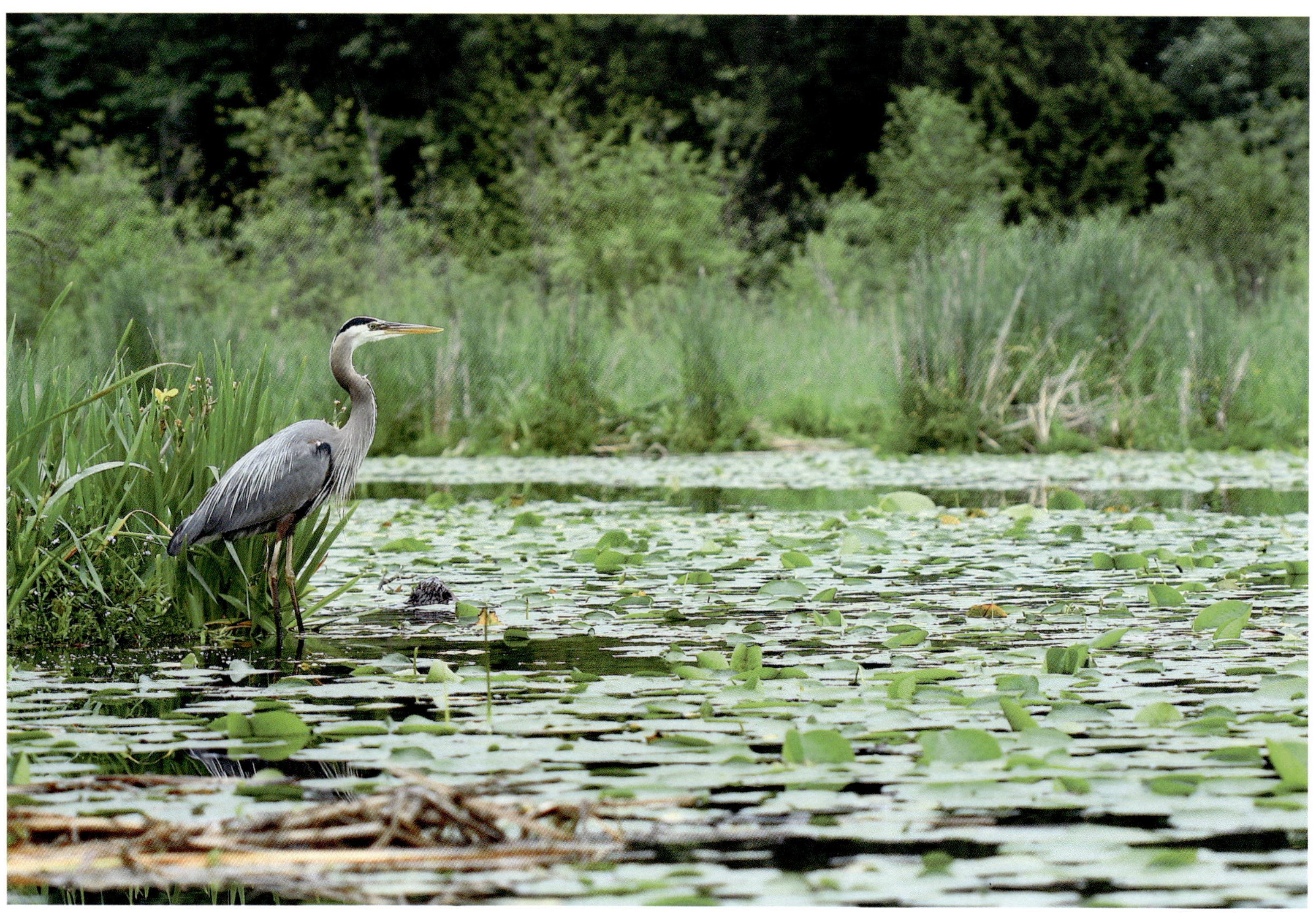

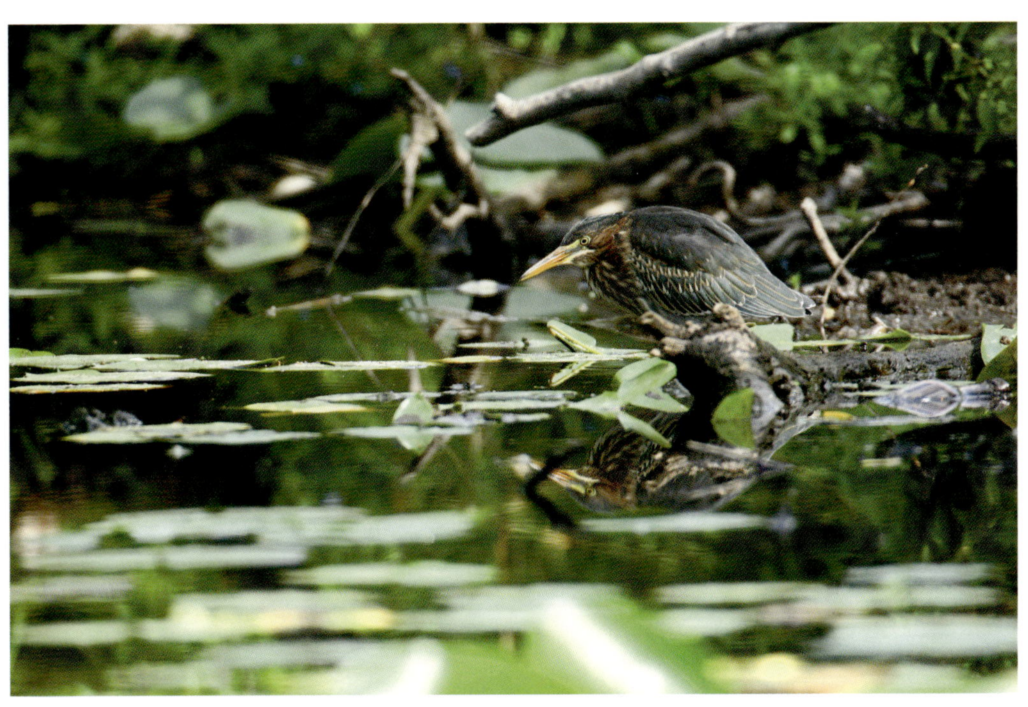

As hundreds of cars inch across the 520 floating bridge every morning and evening, I wonder how many drivers realize that they are only yards away from people strolling through a quiet green wonderland or canoeing among hidden coves and marshy islands, marveling over many thousands of species of trees, plants, birds, and animals.

Do they know that it is possible to create a park in the heart of a modern city that protects over a hundred endangered plants and is home to a stunning variety of birds and woodland and wetland wildlife? Have they thought about how important extending the natural beauty that surrounds our city into its densest areas is to the lifestyle that we so value here in Seattle?

Perhaps not. But I believe that more people than ever before are coming to appreciate the importance of cherishing and celebrating special places such as the Arboretum right on their doorstep. The chance to explore such a diverse natural landscape, from wetlands to mature woodland, is a remarkable introduction to the larger scenery of Washington—and beyond. Certainly the Arboretum shows what can be achieved when parks and wild spaces are part of the vision for urban development.

There are many academic studies that investigate the benefits of parks and natural areas to the health of our communities and our children. I think the proof is easy to find, simply by turning off the highway, getting out of your car, and spending a little time ambling along the pathways that meander from tree-shade into the reeds and cattails of this hidden treasure.

The Arboretum and its wetlands are an amazing asset to our region, and one we should try to build on. This book is a testament to what can be achieved when people join together to conserve a place they love, and a challenge to our modern urban planners—a park should be so much more than a patch of grass and a swing set!

— Roger Hoesterey

Vice President and Regional Director, The Trust for Public Land

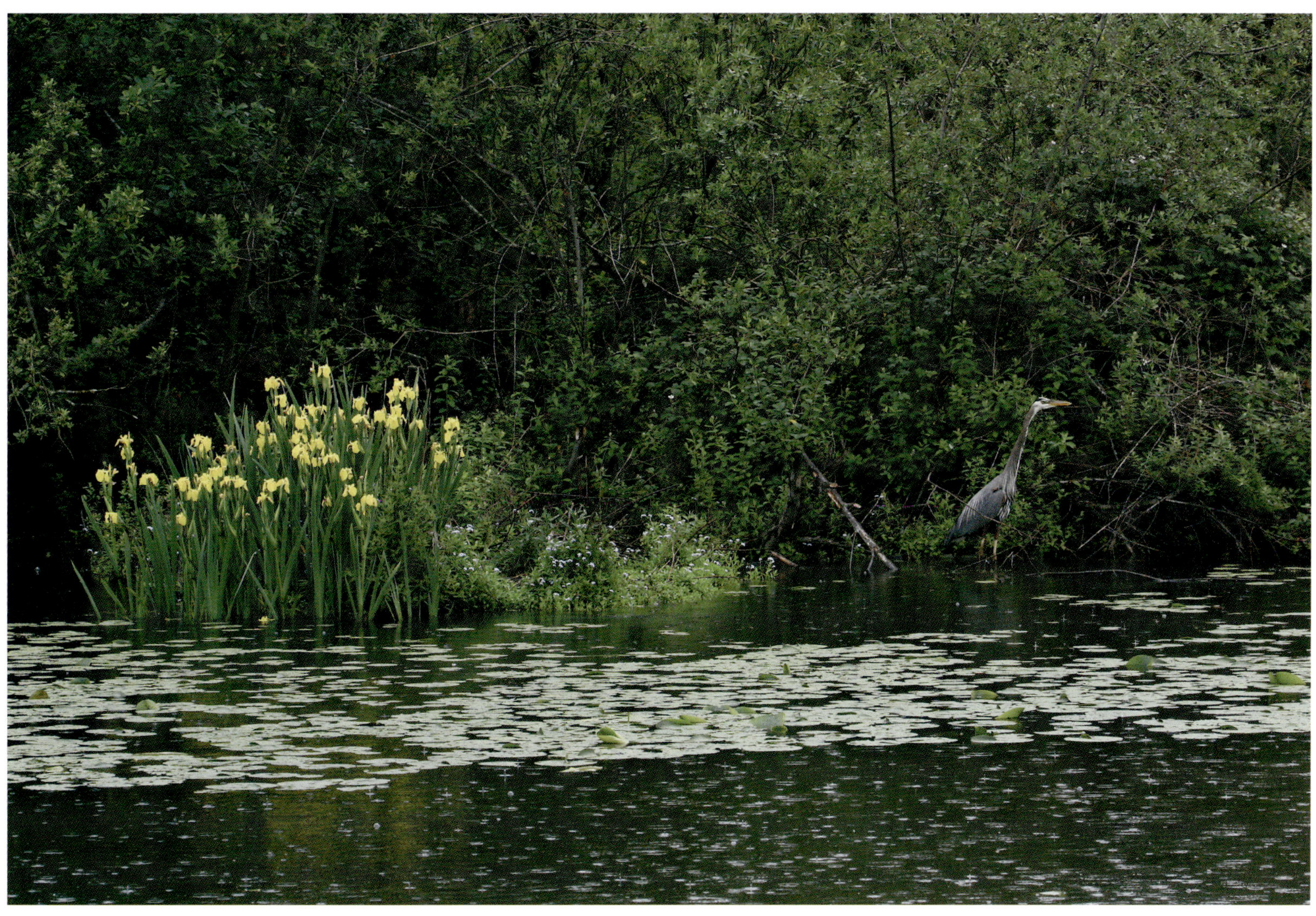

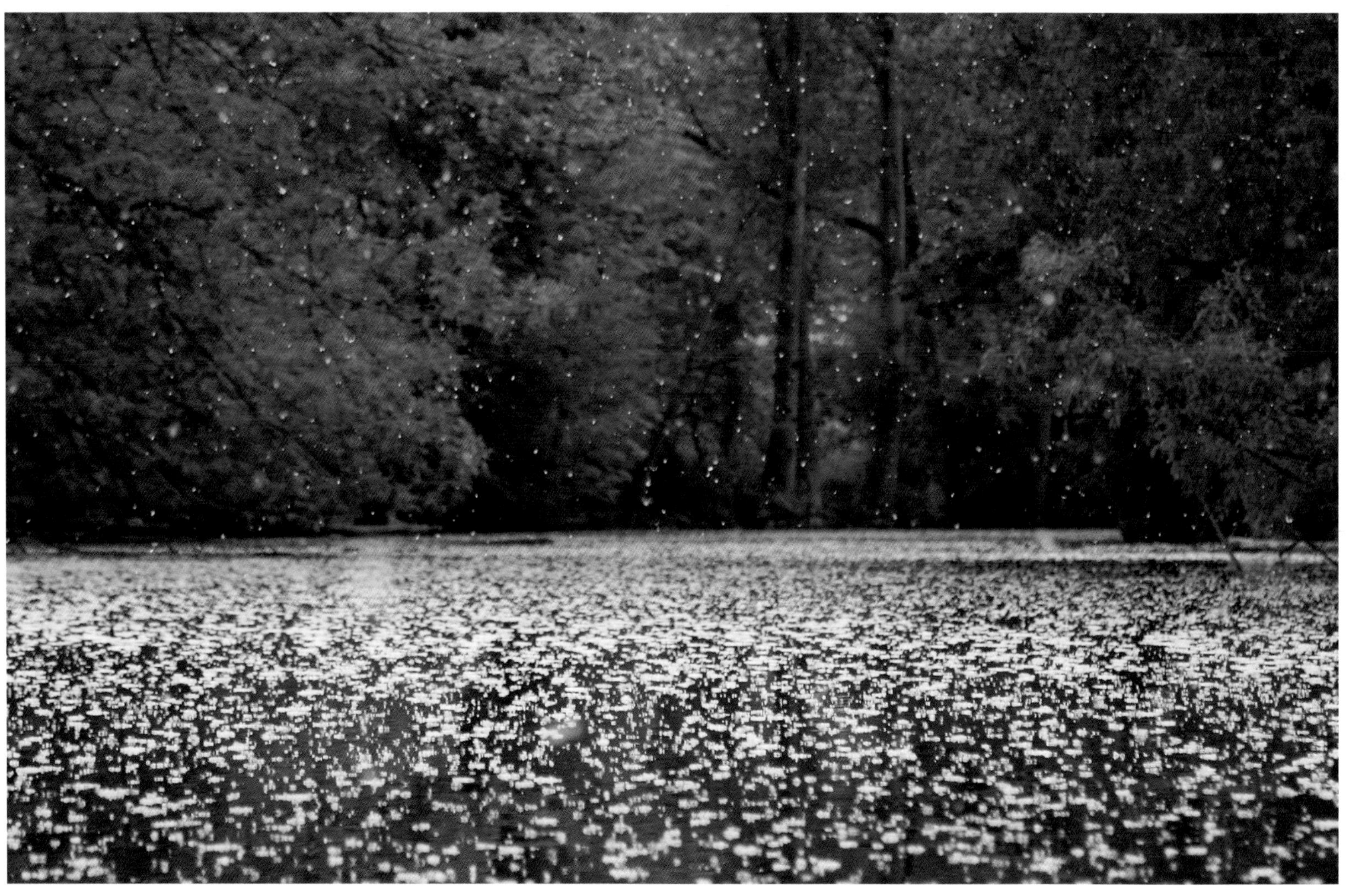

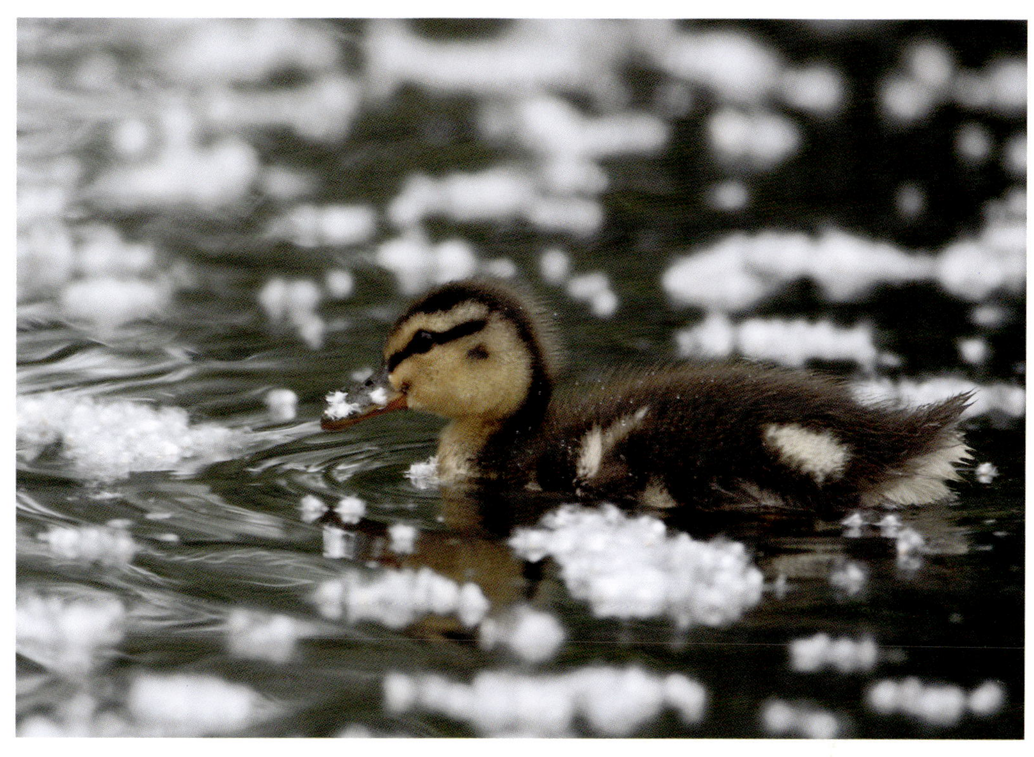

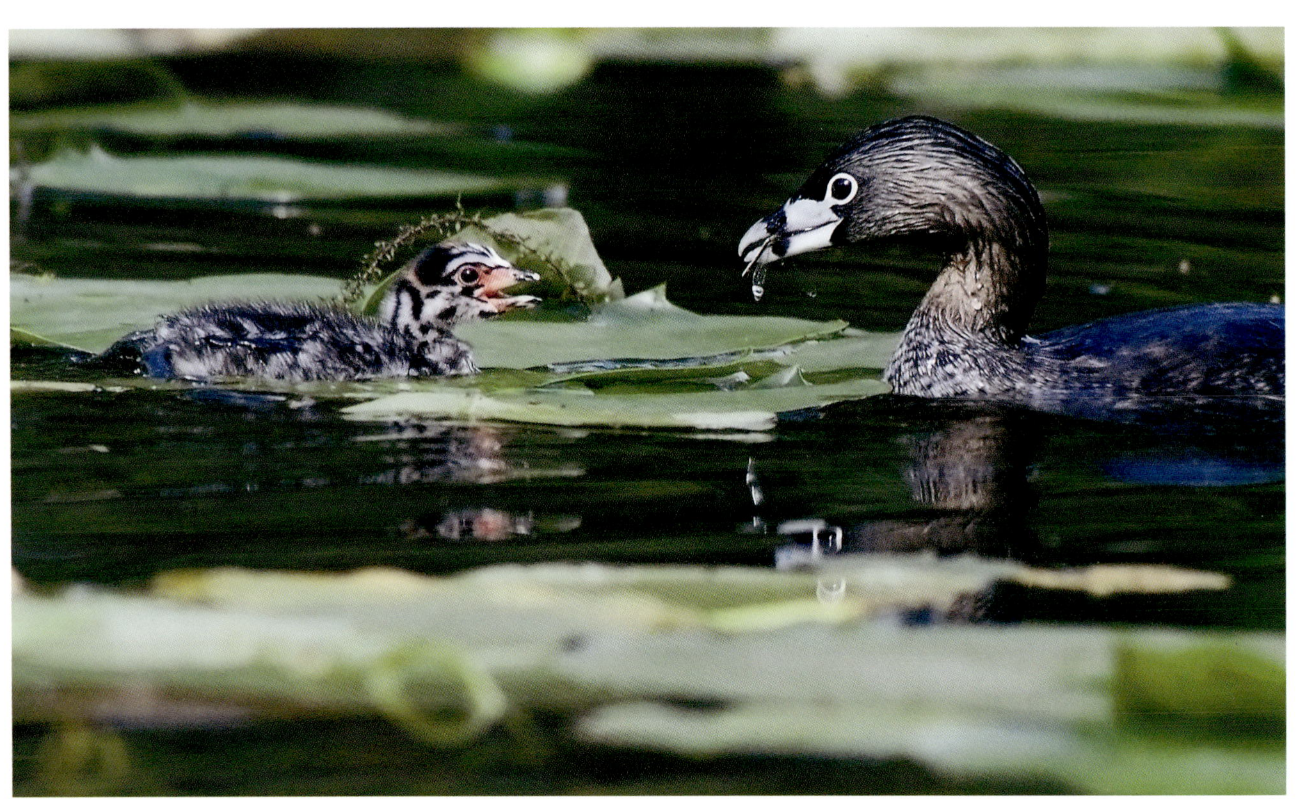

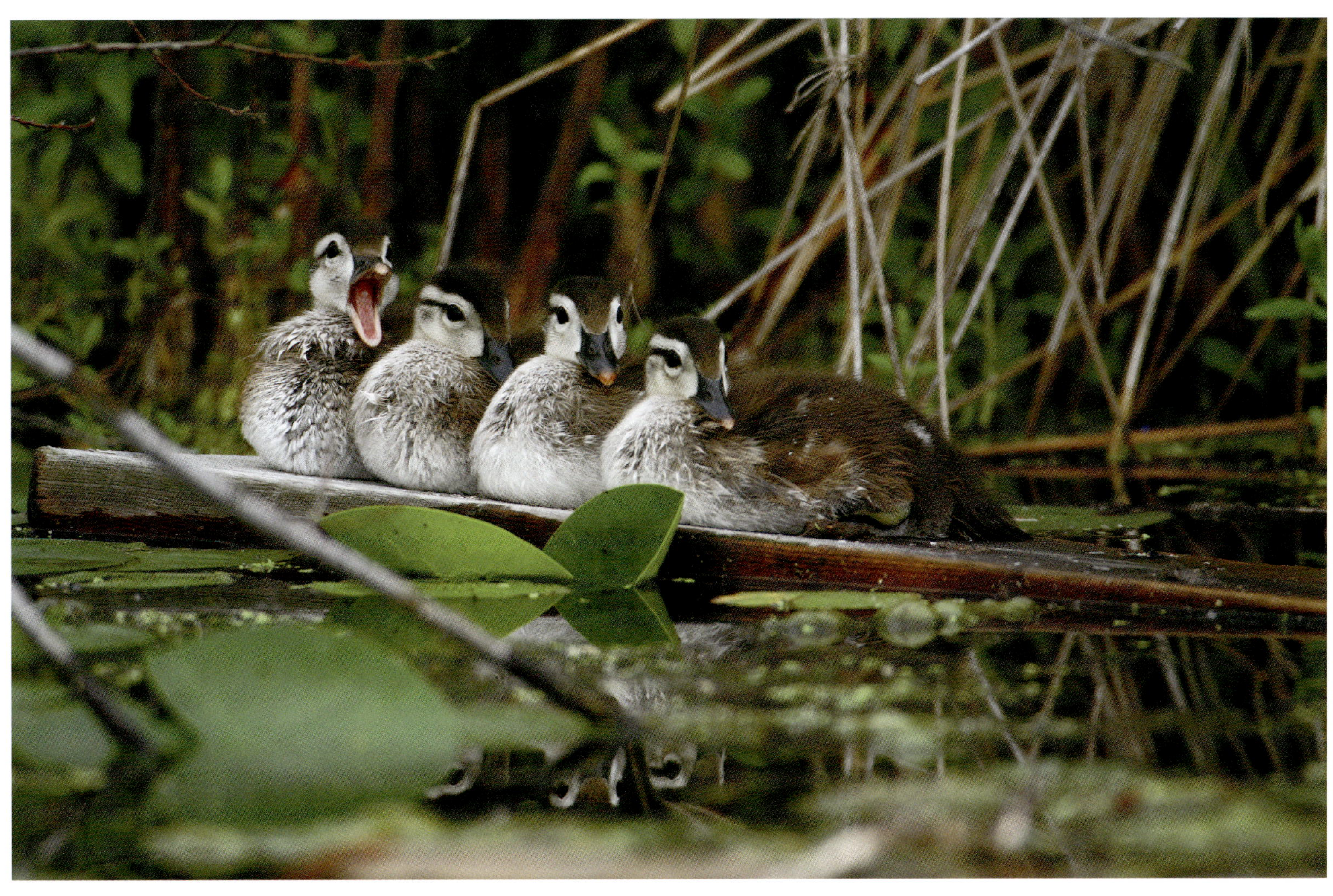

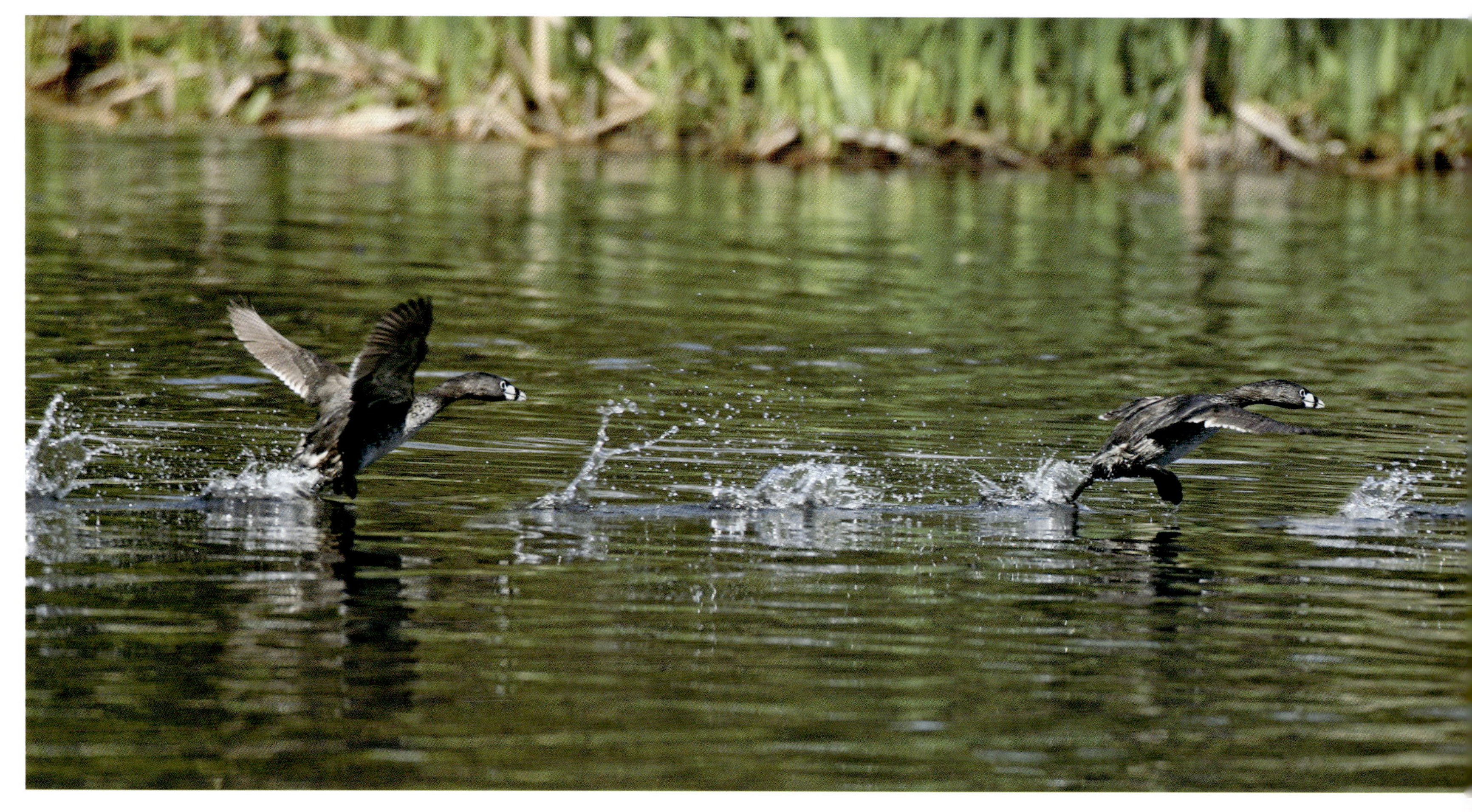

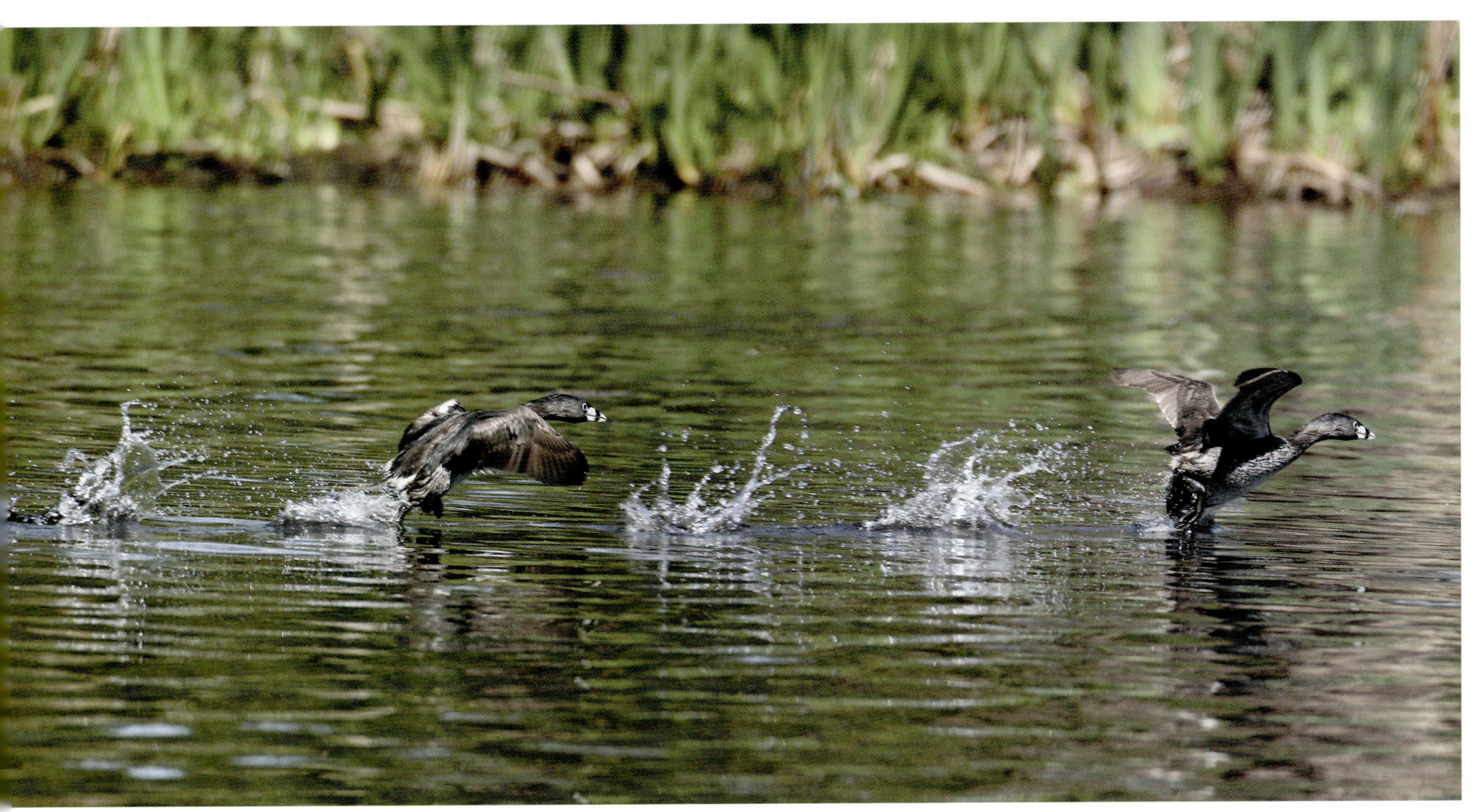

Sun-day More-ning in the Land of the Wetly Wet and Greenly Green with a Child and an Old April Fool

Slickers and brellas and Wellies well on, smushed we into the deep foolish joy of Sprang coming fastly now in the jigglesome muckety muck where the Smiley-wily Things are. And found Smiley-wily Things indeed!

The upsplashing spears of highris splunching holes in the fairy air. The wallowing willy-pads. The coiling tails of the cats-to-be. Egglings hidden in the blunderbushes. Great globs of amfibbyous much-lucious grawling with imphant insects—the dandyprats, smiders, milly-poodles, mini-frish, plumblebees, teeny-tiny crockojaws and the wonder-water wiggles.

Herd we the krill of the Great-Willed White Spork, the smuddy thud of the Stagnating Spoon, and the chortle of the blue-nosed Bibby Bird, crying "*lunch-bucket, lunch-bucket.*"

Smelled we the smelly Things coming in and going back, rising up and razing down as the merry-go-round of lively life goes round.

Felt we the slime, slurred we the ooze, and shrugged the sticky-wicky as it catched and clawed to hold us still. And all the while, all the while, the Wet came down, the Wet rose up, the Wet roused round and round making us all wildly wet. But cared not, we!

For we were green where grows the greening. Oh, there's that green and that green and still another green and a greener green over there, and out there the green that's greener than that, and the most prodijus green of all right here nearby. And we smunched some greens in our flingers and painted our noses and clothes and toes all green to go home green. And oh how we did that! Home again, home again, wetly and greenly and lively were we.

Yes, yes!

Two trioophant captains of the explodition into the deeply foolish joy of Sprang.

— *Robert Fulghum*

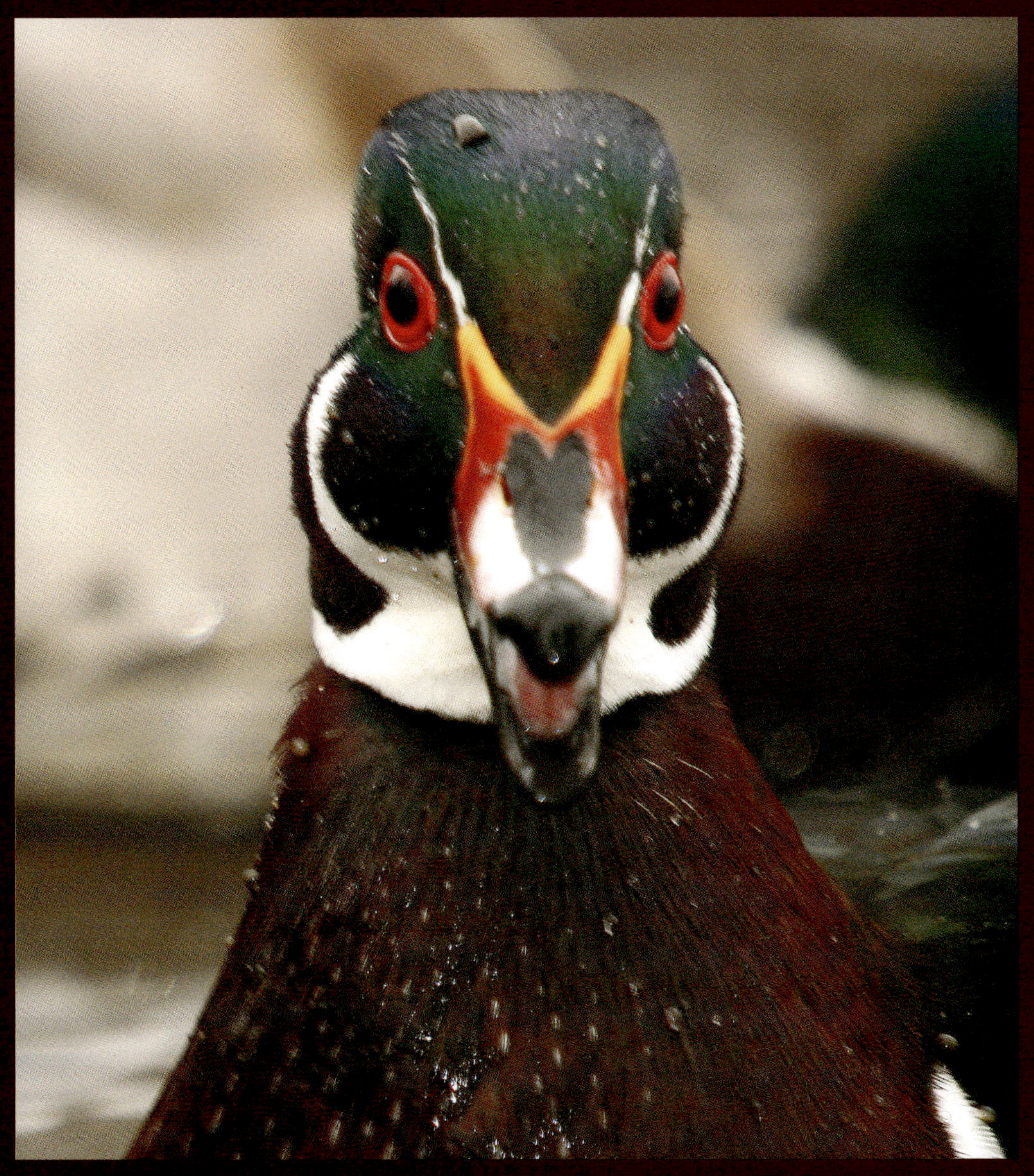

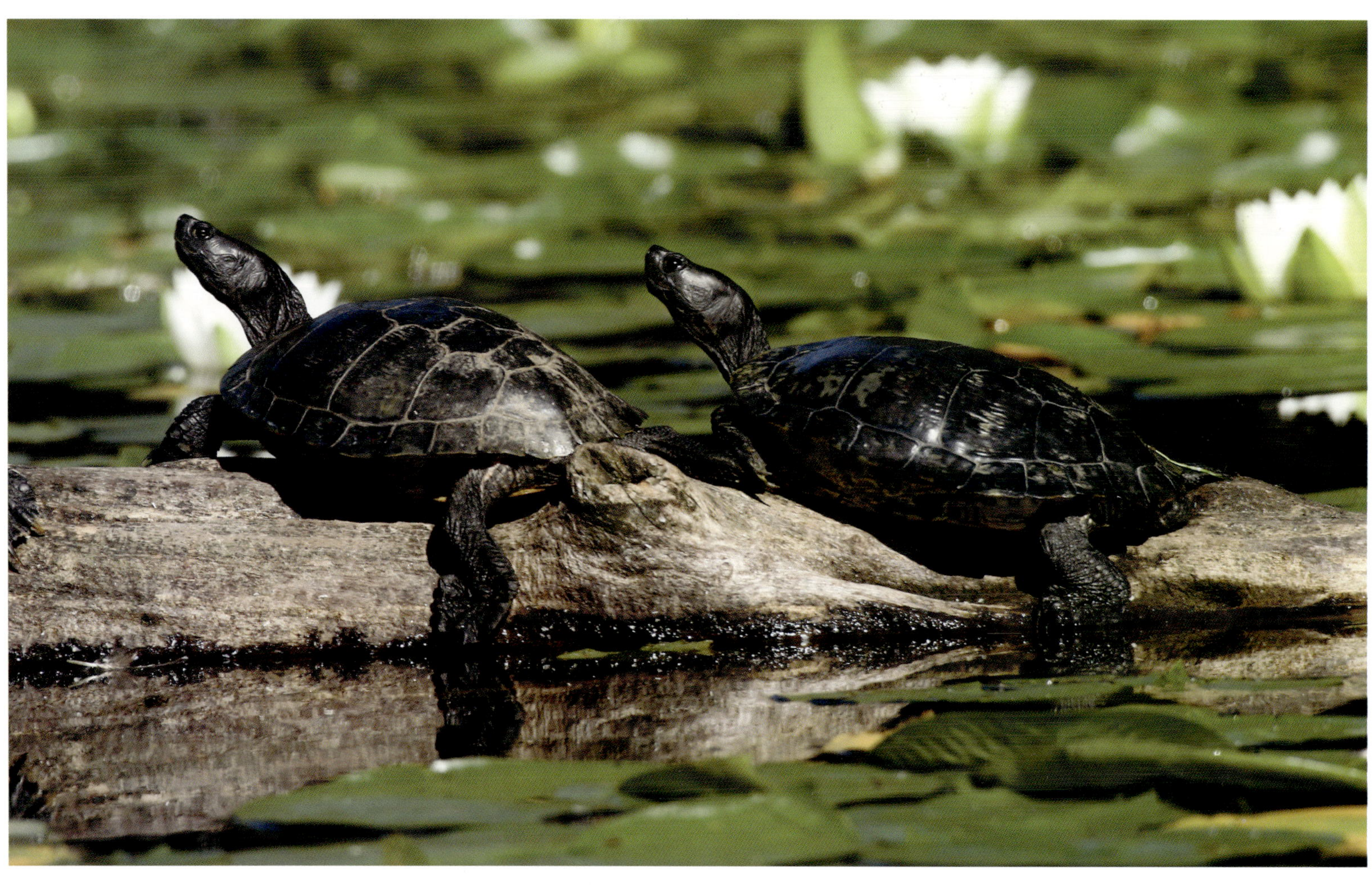

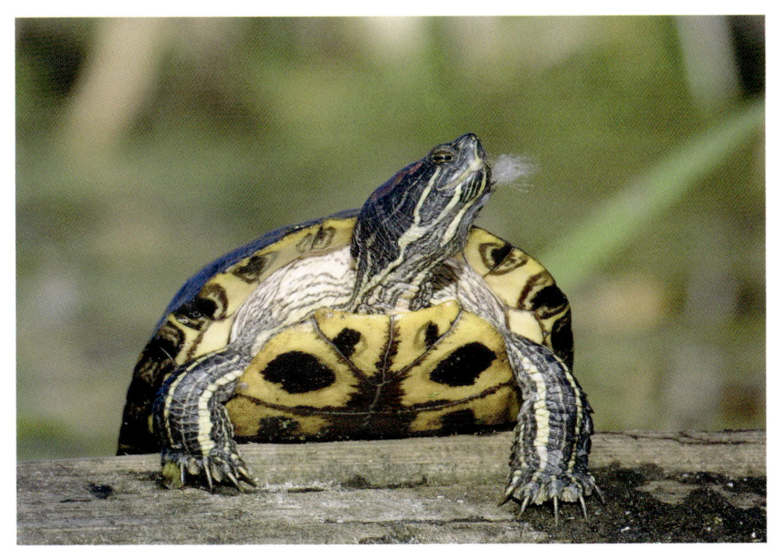

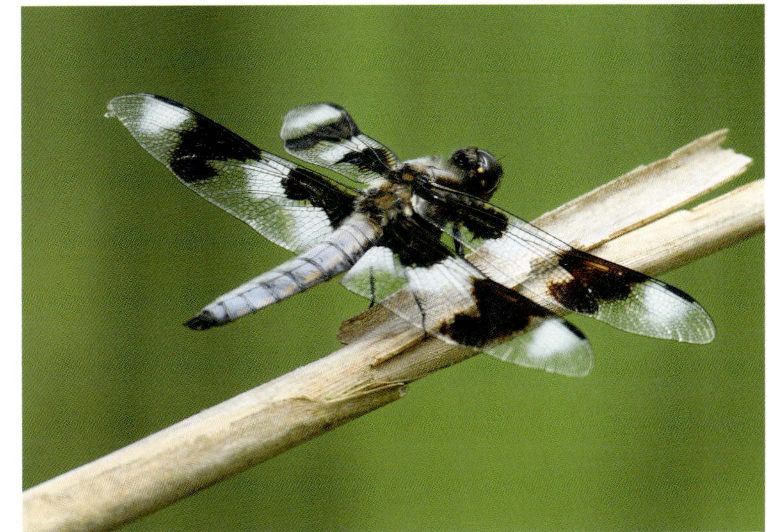

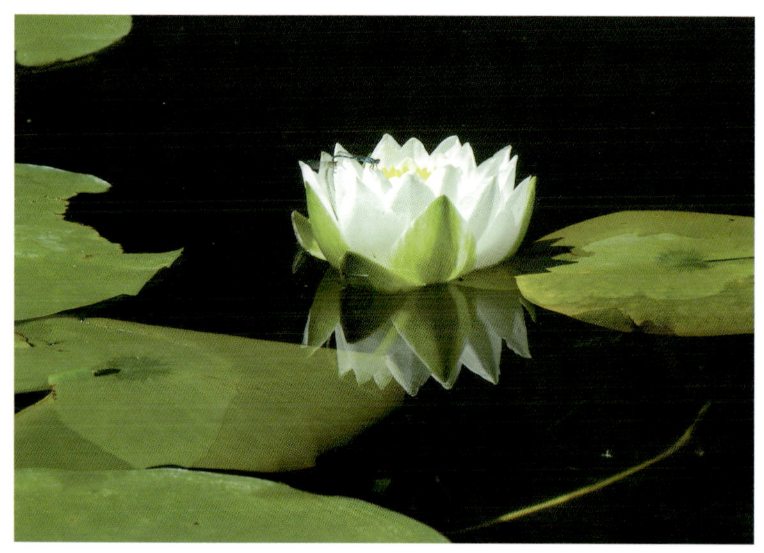

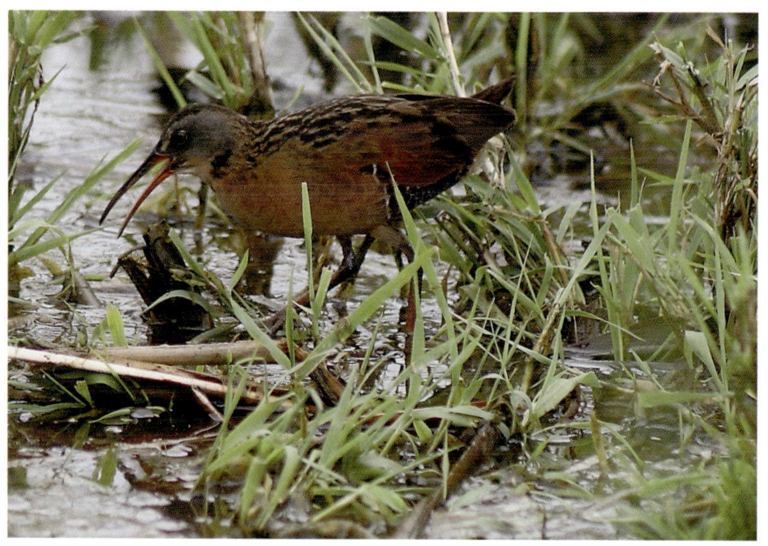

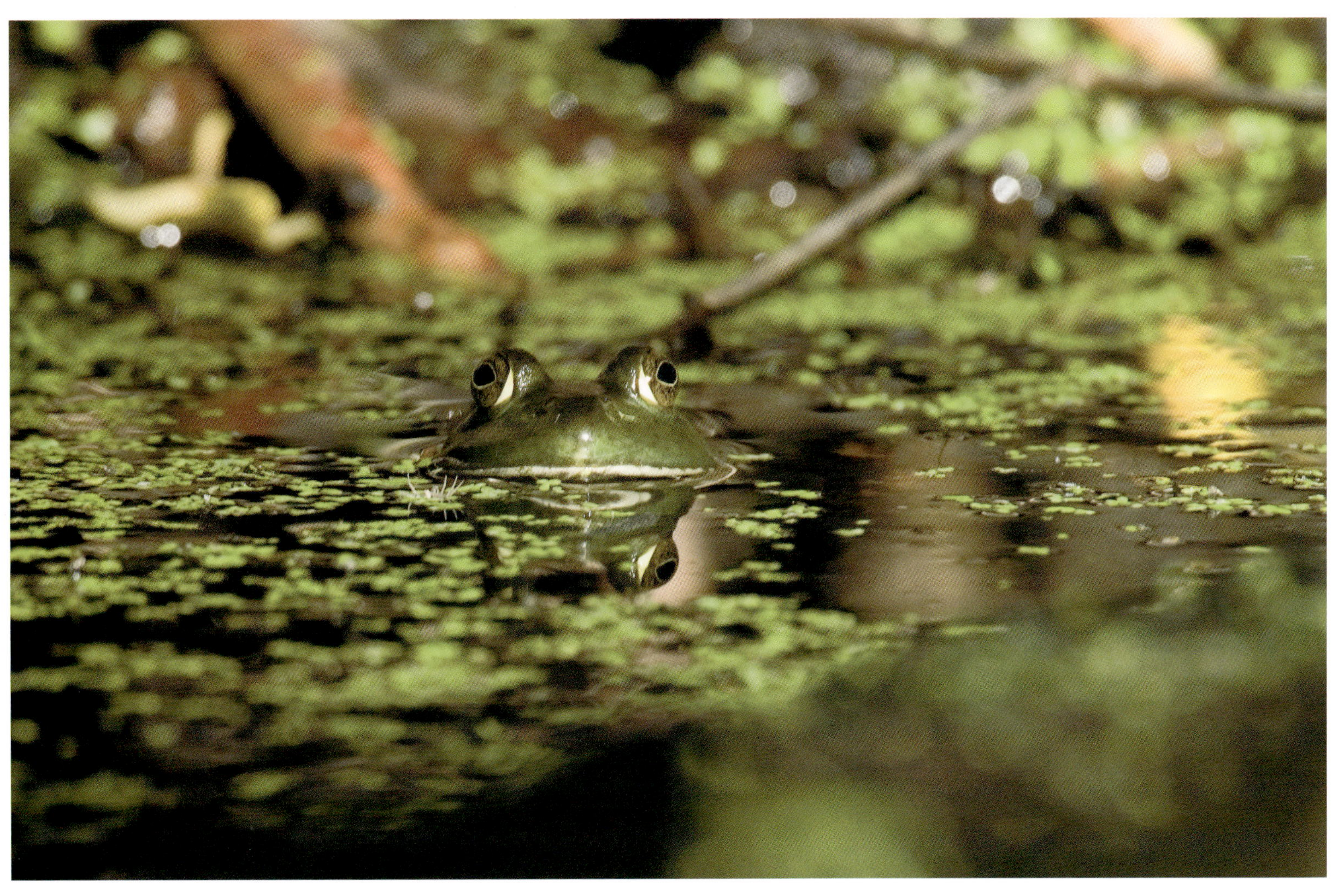

Like many present and former Seattleites, I have had a casual acquaintance with the Arboretum wetlands: a glimpse of a great blue heron standing solitary vigil as drivers pass by on Highway 520; a pleasant winter's walk on Foster Island when the rest of the Arboretum was "out of bloom"; or a place to canoe during the summer.

Becoming involved in the Wild Within project changed my perspective from casual to intimate. During 2006, I spent an average of four hours a week in the wetlands: kayaking, walking, observing, and photographing. What became clear to me is the scope and natural diversity in this small pocket of Seattle's urban fabric.

The marsh and its resident herons are easily recognized pieces of the wetland quilt. Listen and you will hear the ratcheting call of the marsh wren and see its amazing football-shaped nest woven from cattail reeds. Near water's edge noisy, colorful woodpeckers and flickers thrive, along with black-capped chickadees and tiny bushtits. Tall cottonwoods serve as lookout posts for bald eagles and red-tailed hawks watching for their next meal. Resident beavers leave their mark throughout the wetlands, including an impressive lodge clearly visible from the shore. These pieces are woven together with plants such as bog iris, salmonberry, snowberry, willow, and alder.

Everywhere you look, there is something to see. And hear. And smell. And feel.

It was the looking that changed the Arboretum wetlands from acquaintance to friend. Instead of rushing through on my way to someplace else, I took the time to truly look at, breathe in, and really see what was right in front of me. In doing so, I learned that some of the most magical creatures and fantastic places can be found as close as an urban wetland.

— *Michele A. Burton*

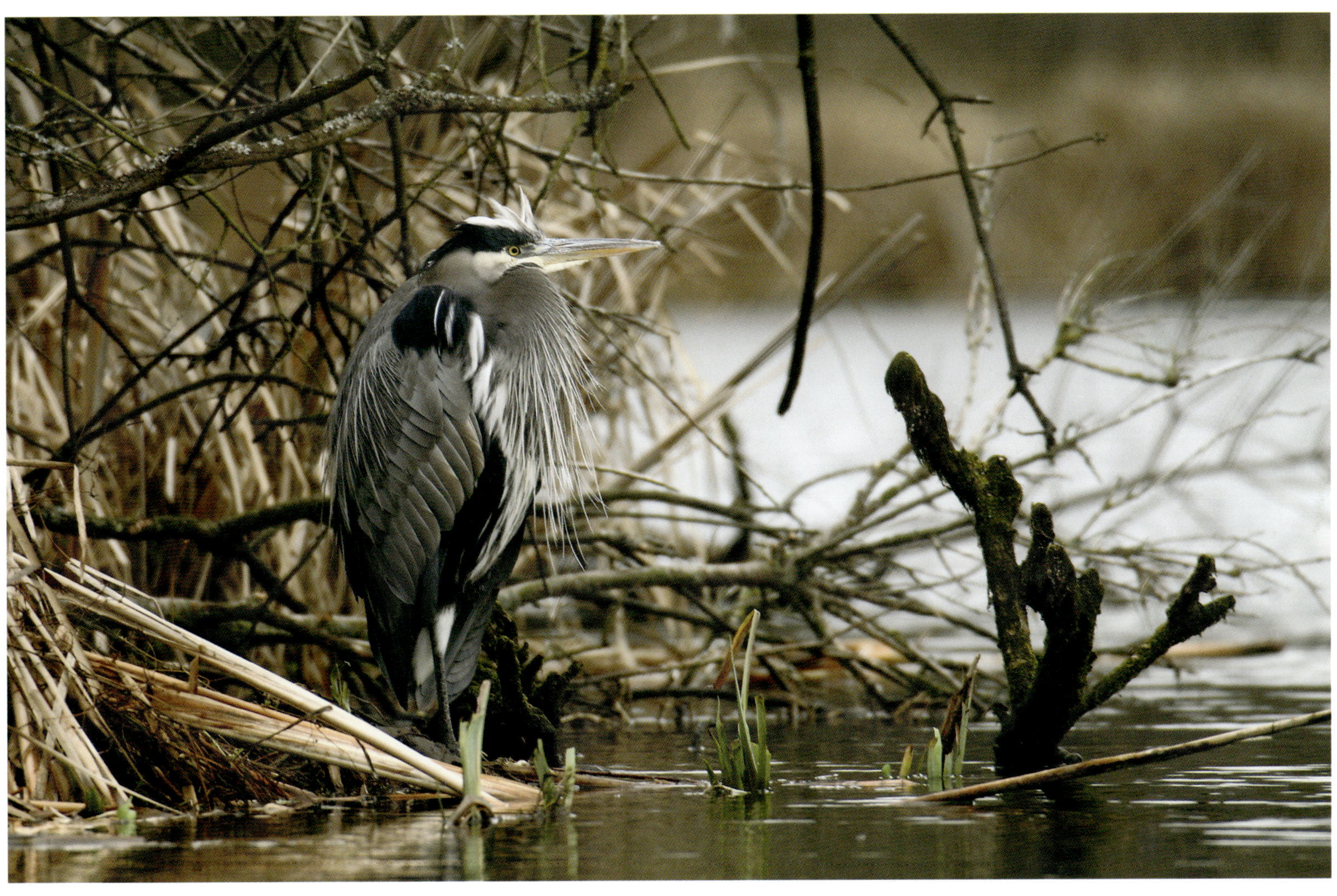

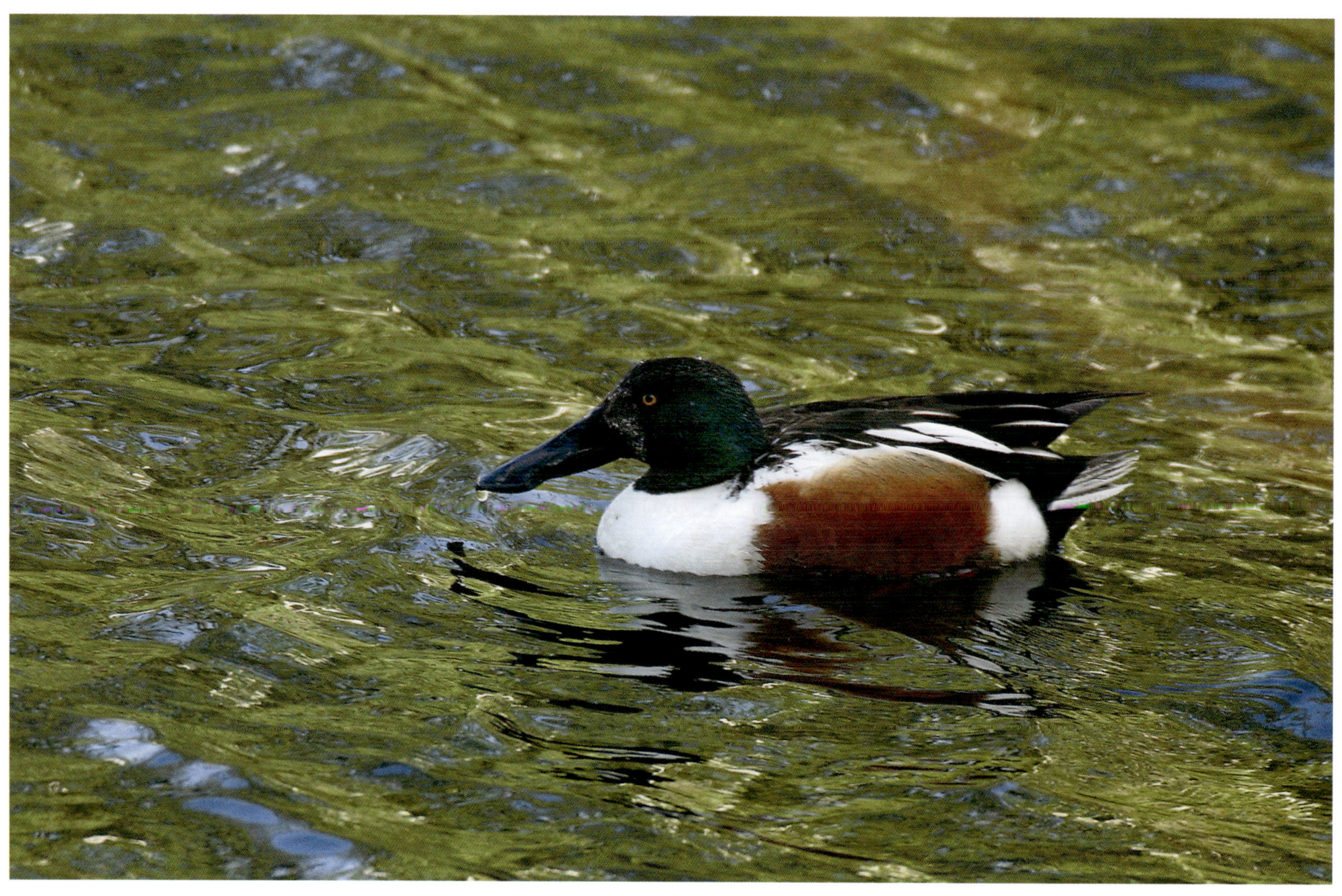

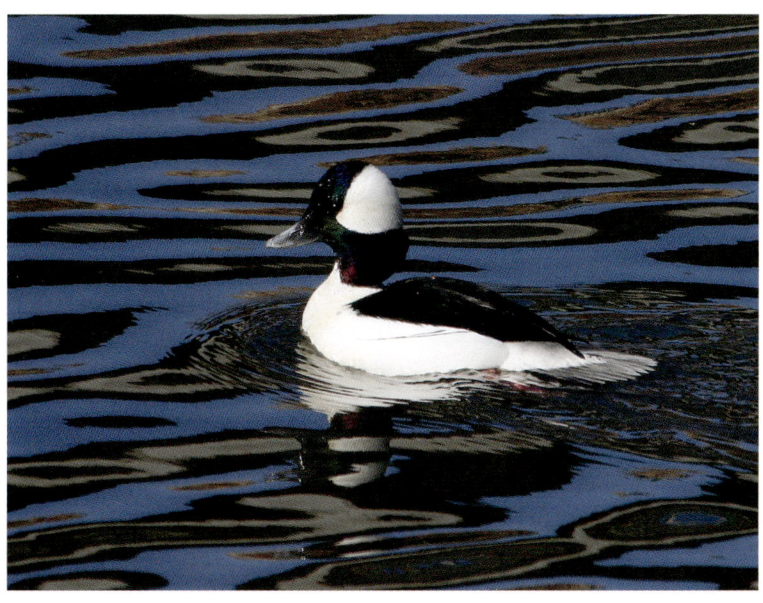

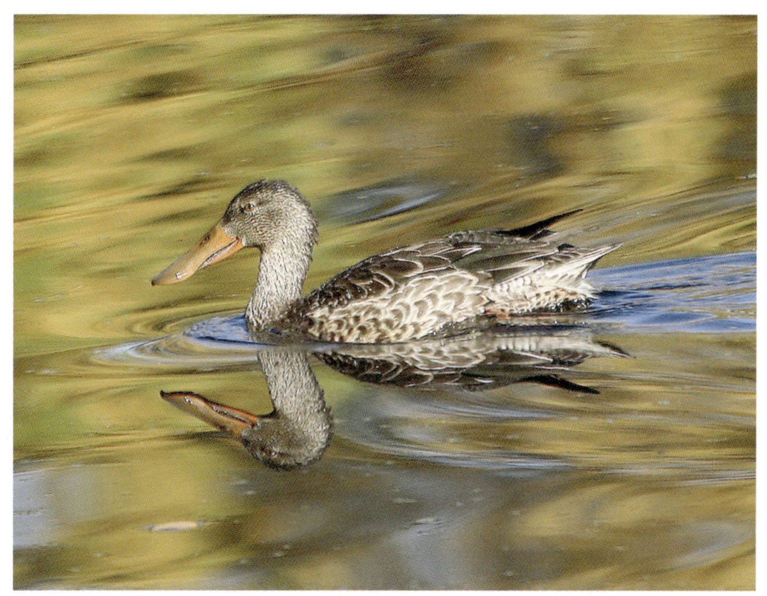

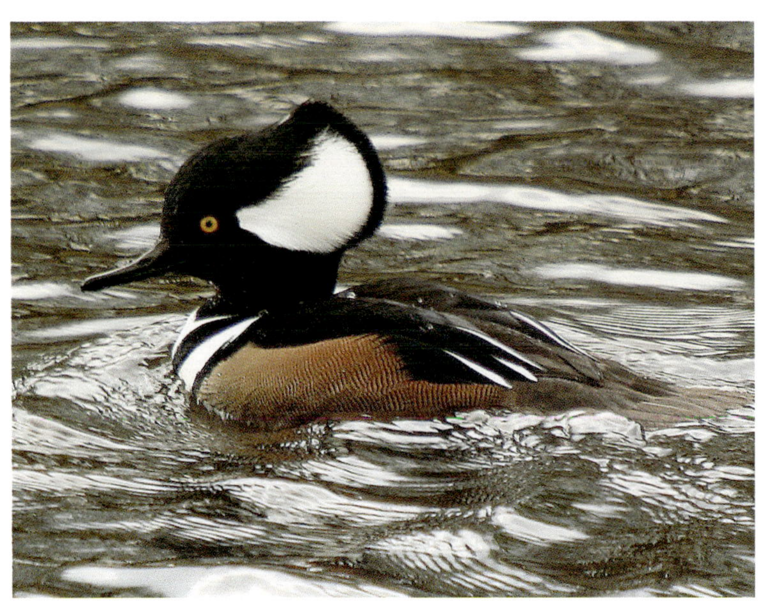

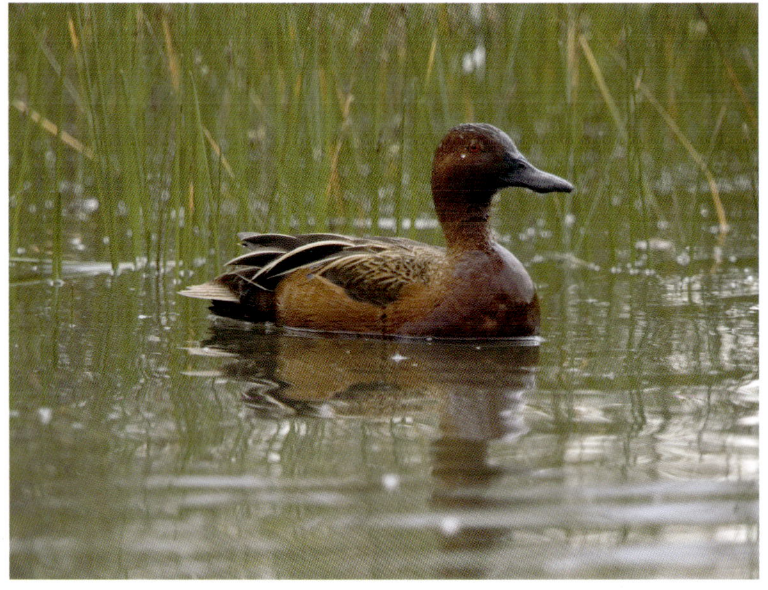

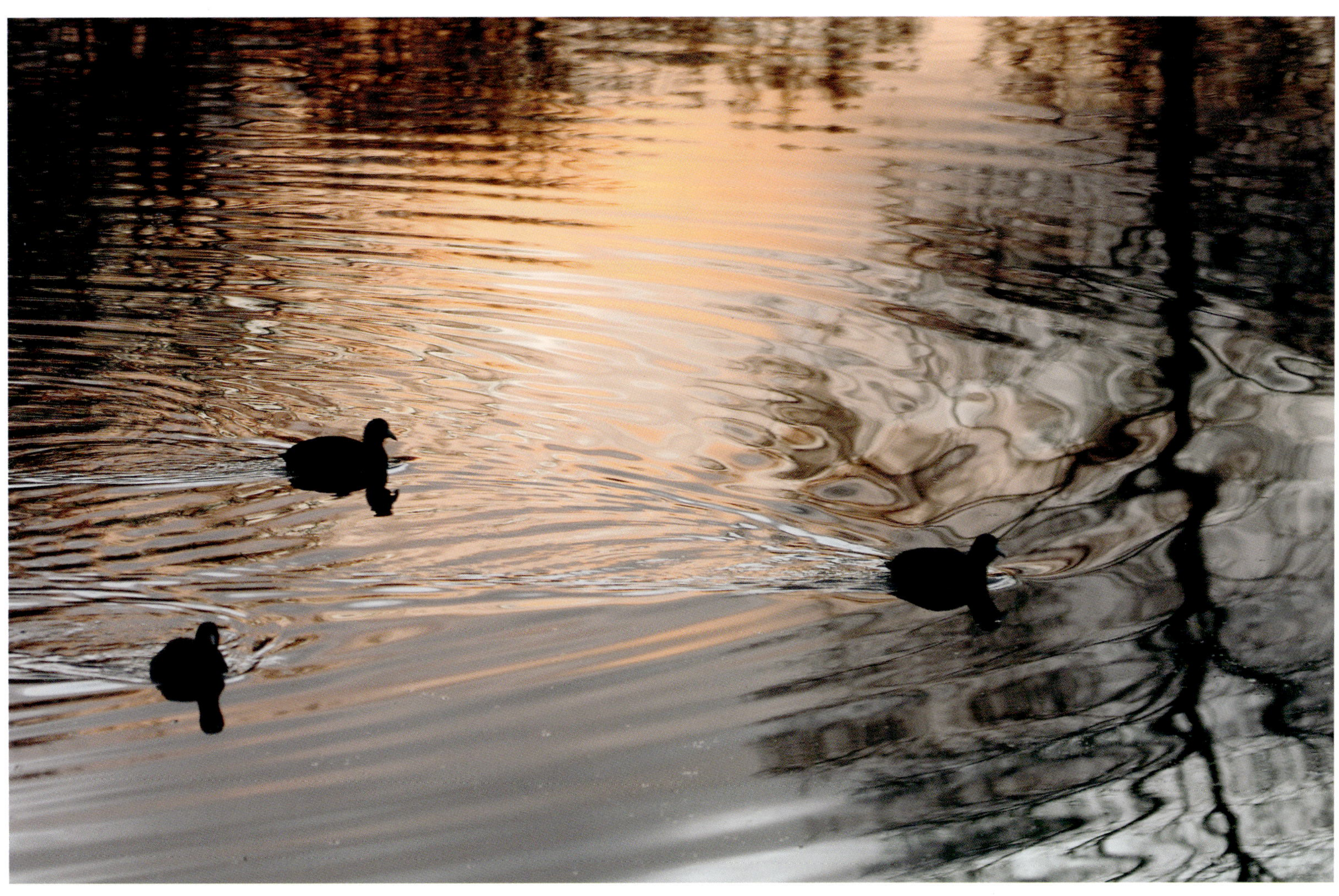

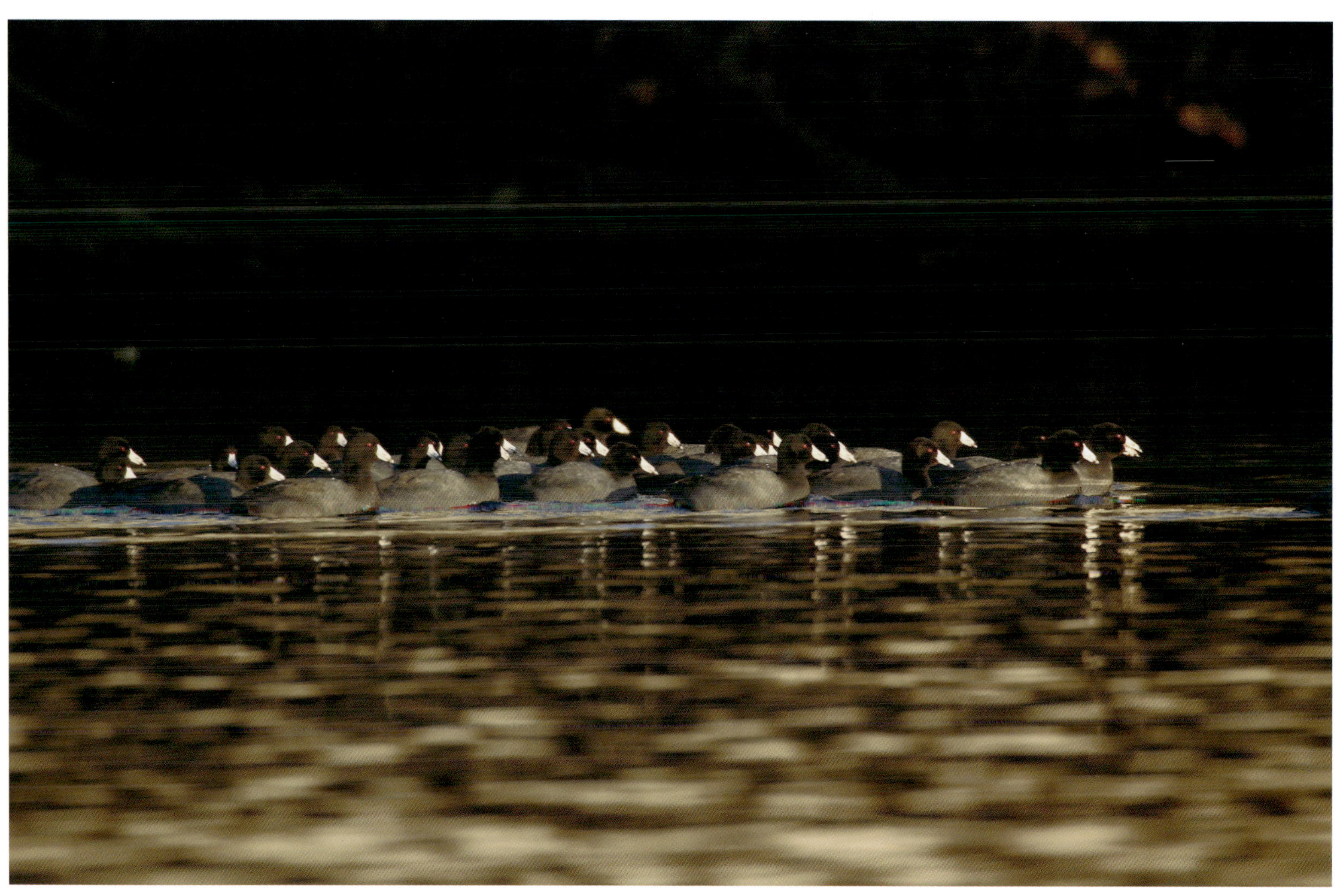

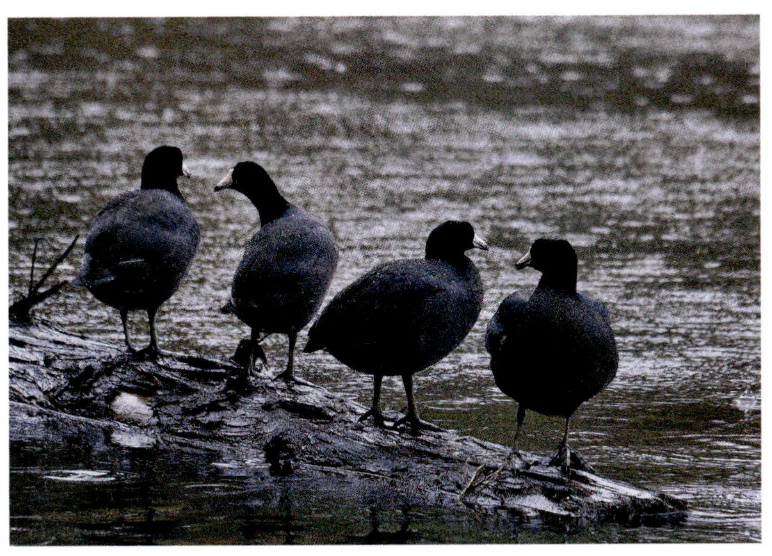

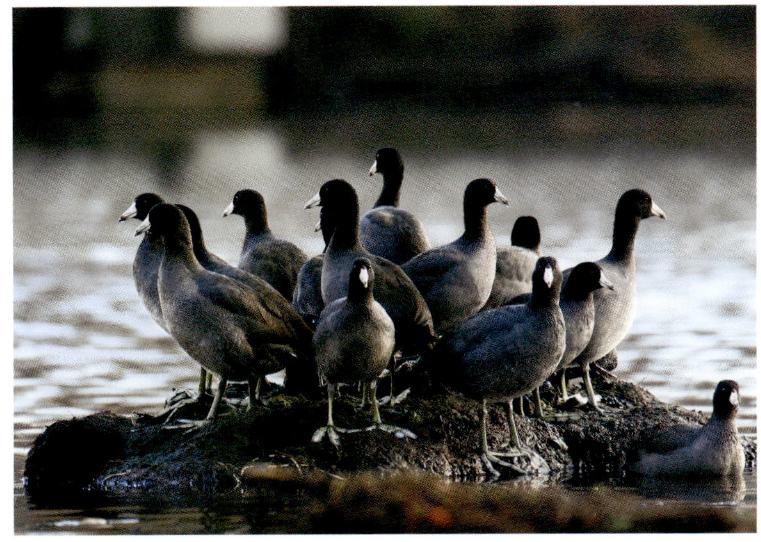

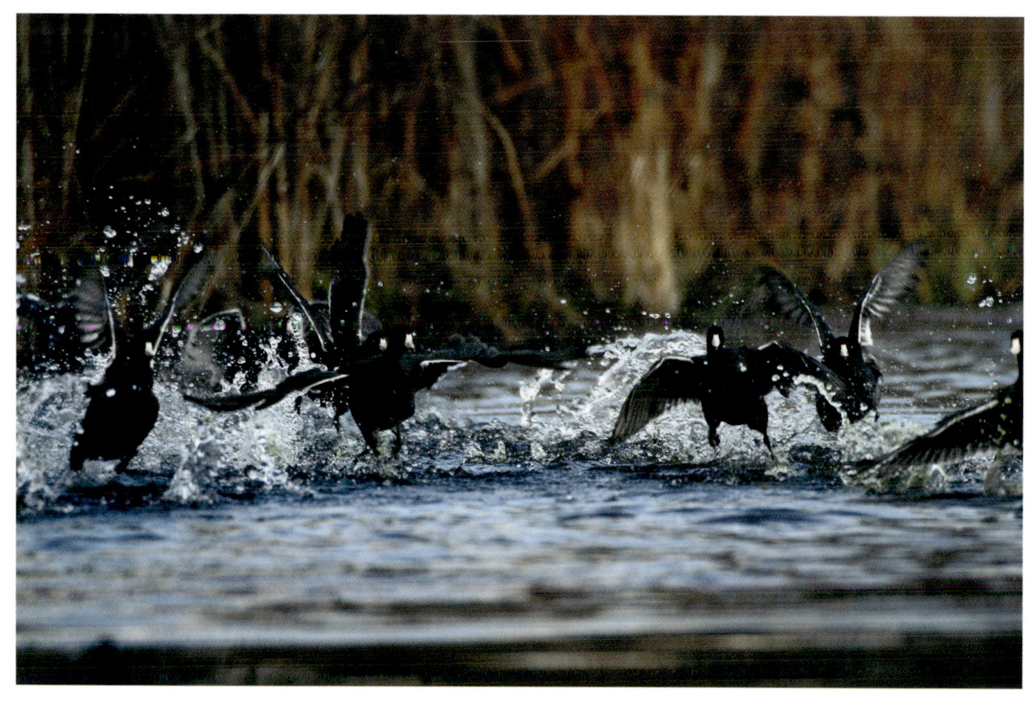

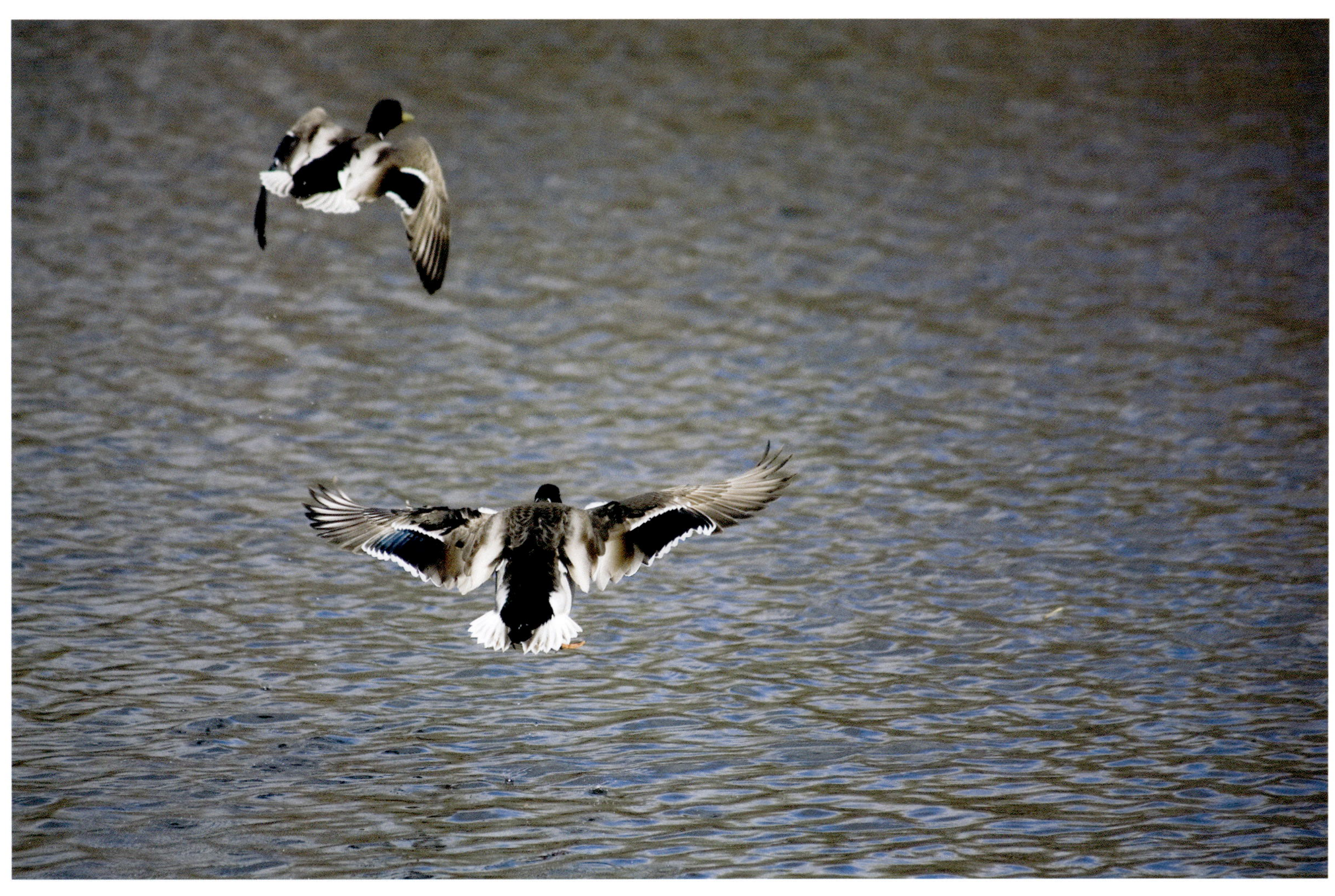

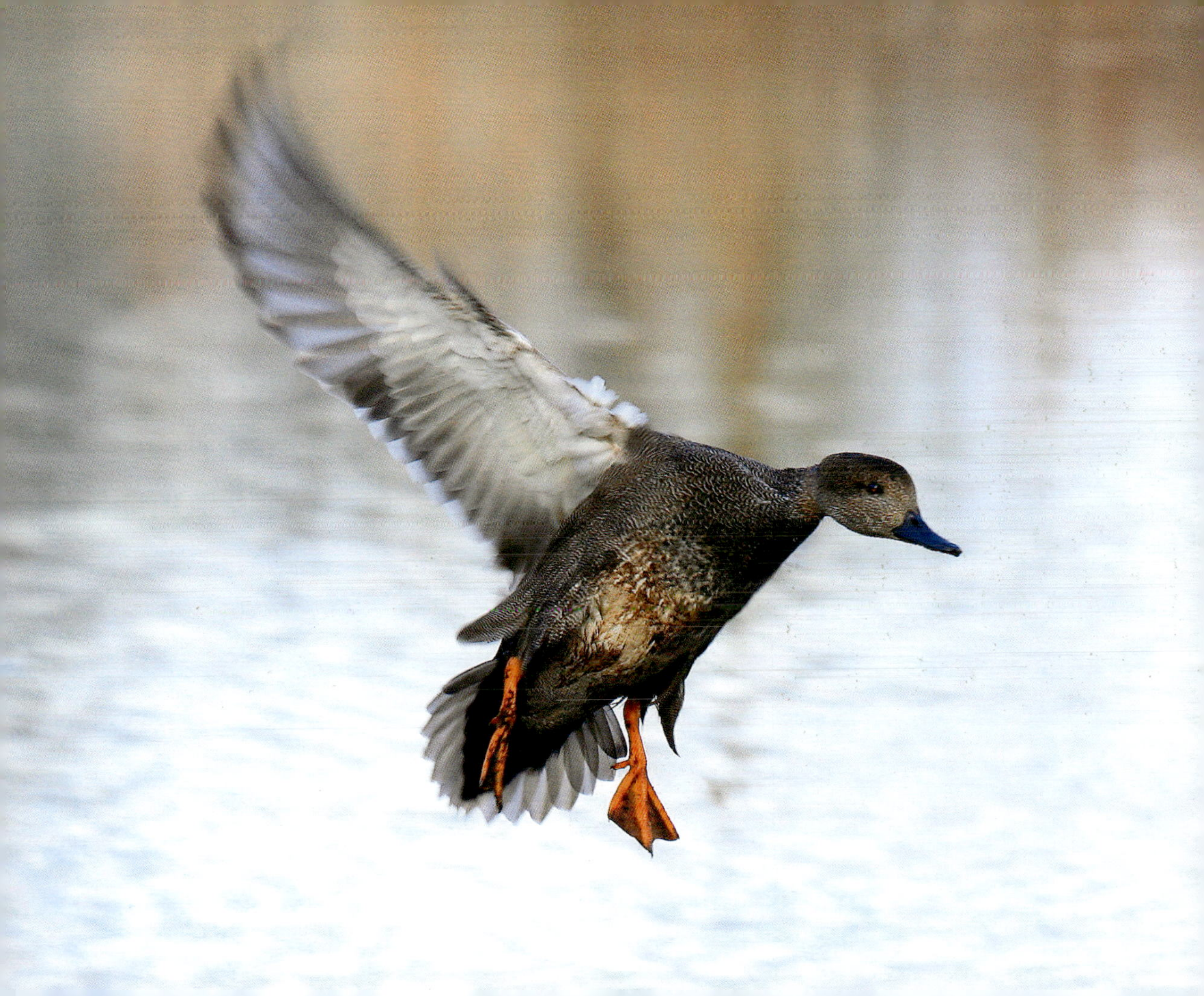

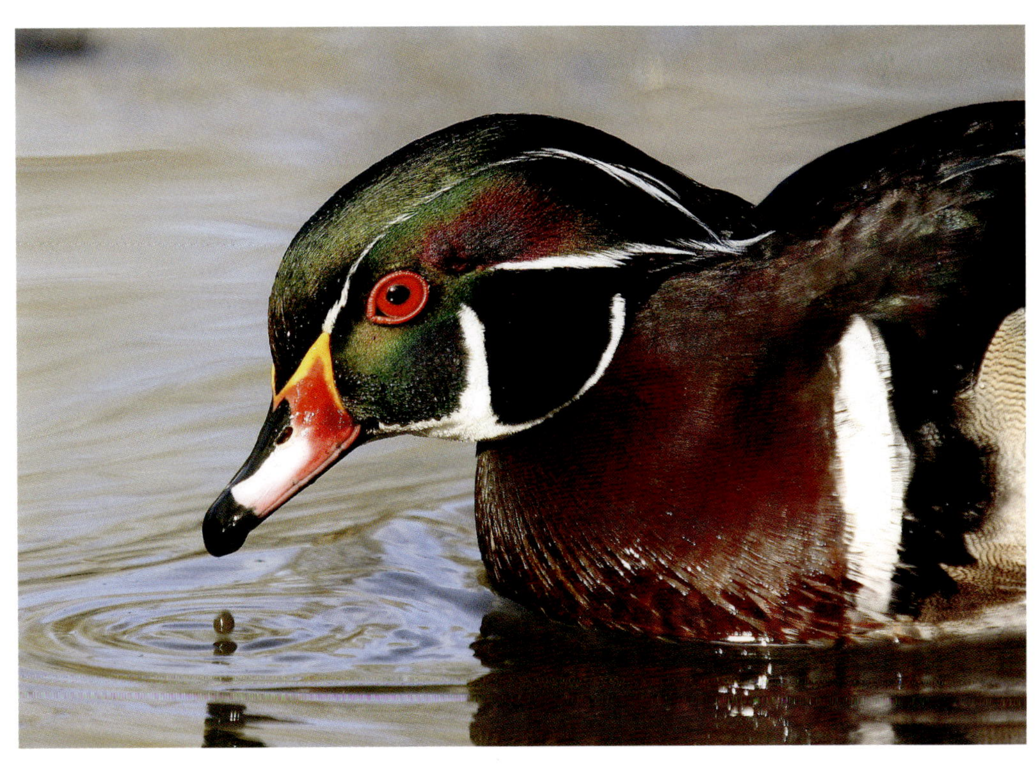

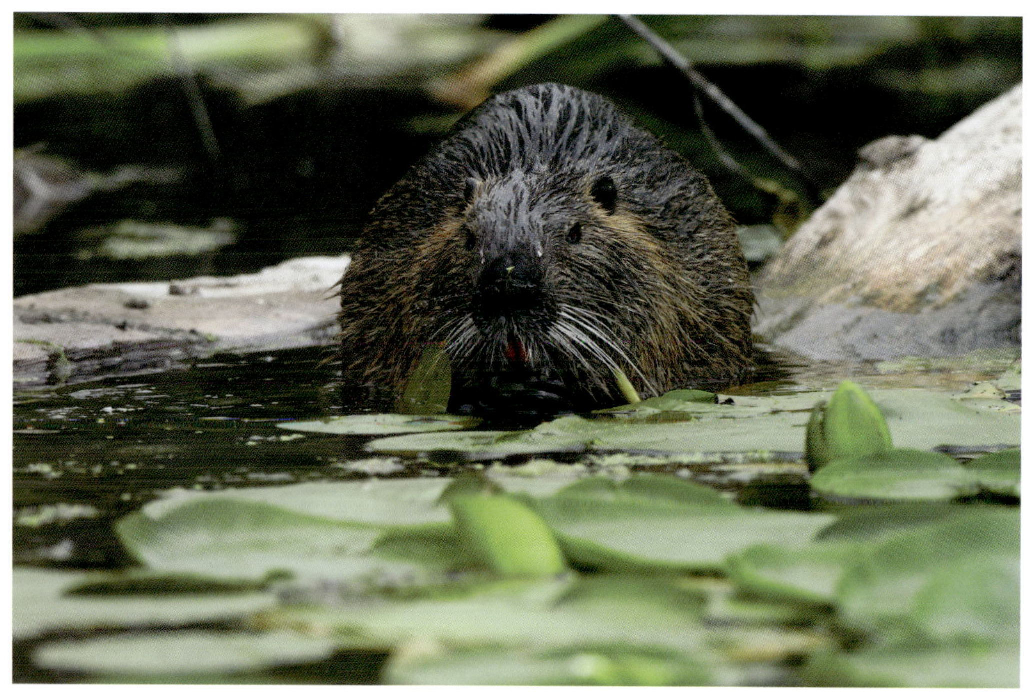

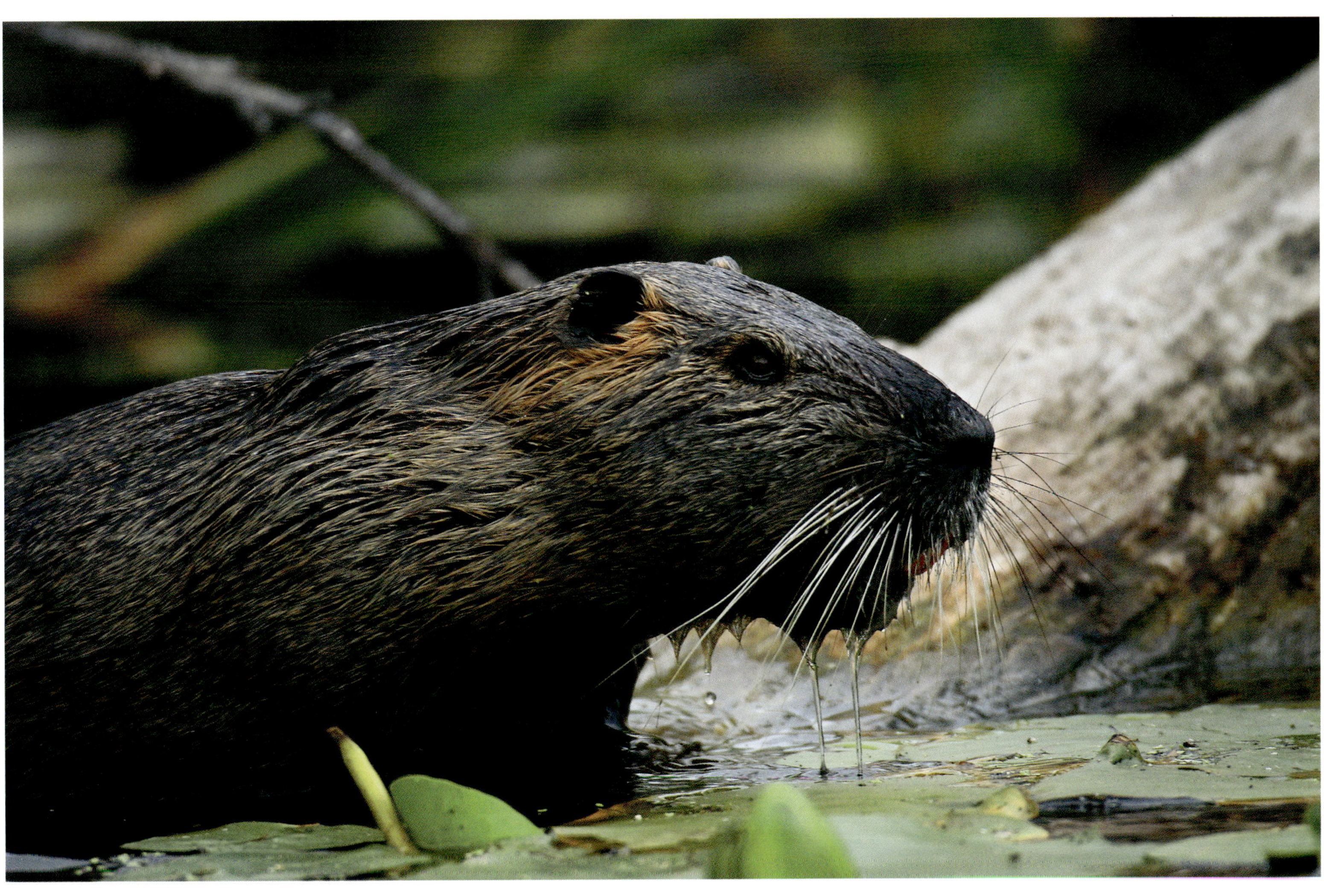

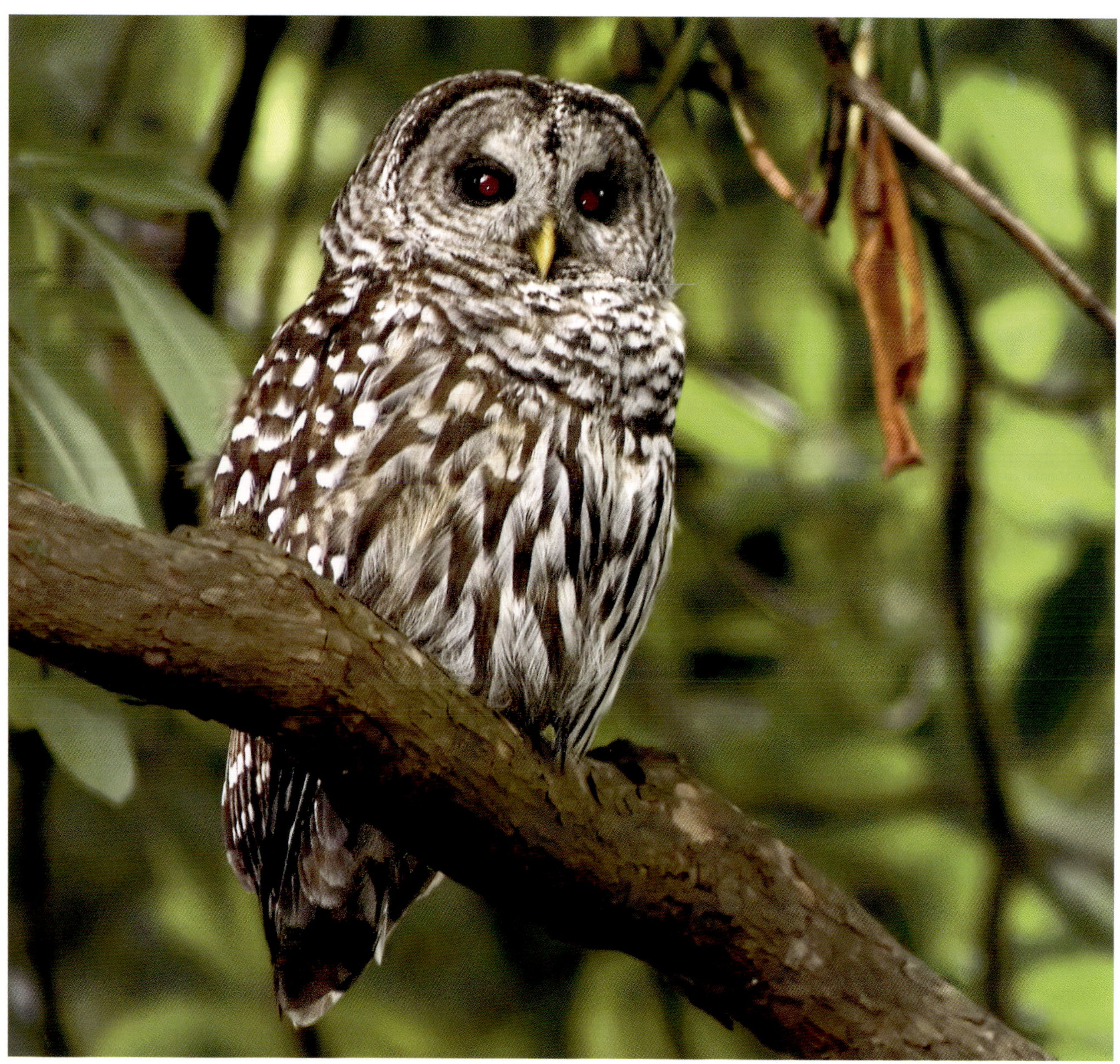

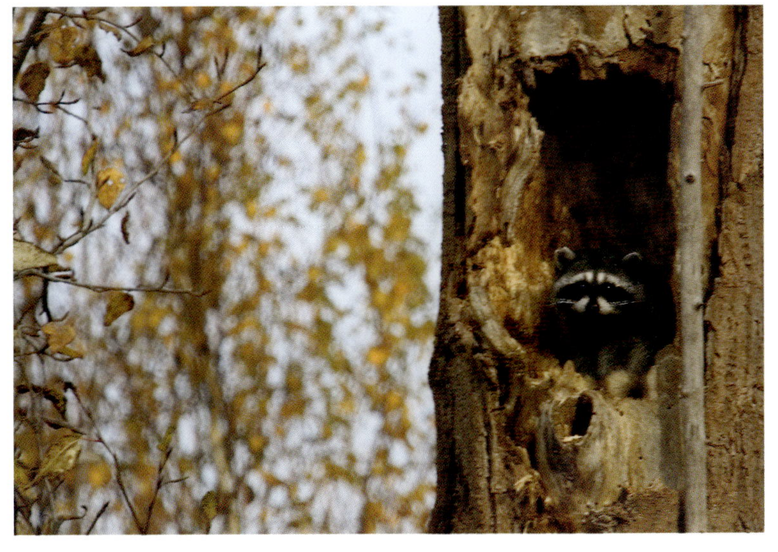

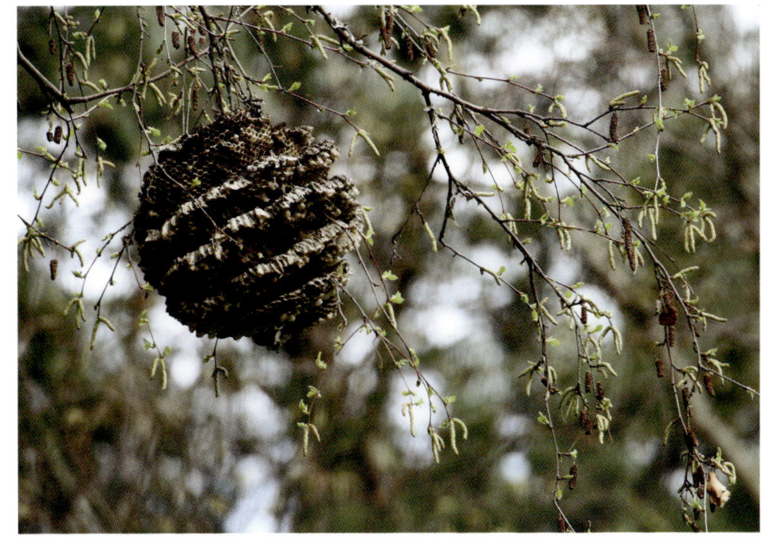

The waters between Foster Island, the 520 bridge, and the Arboretum are a wildlife paradise. Paradoxically, above the sounds of roaring freeway traffic I can hear the honks of Canada geese, the quacks of ducks, the screams of eagles, and the haunting squawks of the great blue heron. Mallards and mergansers skid across the still water, disturbed only slightly by our canoe paddles and not at all by passing trucks and SUVs.

Early on an April Sunday morning, the water is glassy calm. The eastern sunlight colors the new foliage of willows and poplars, and dead cattails along the shoreline. The dark water is so still that reflected concrete pillars supporting the freeway seem to continue down like ancient colonnades.

We are searching for the beaver lodge we saw last fall and evidence that the beavers still inhabit it. It lies only a few feet from the freeway. Old lodges have been abandoned, and new trees and bushes sprout from them, but we see that the active lodge, a mound of mud and branches, has recently cut sticks embedded in it, so they are still here. It would be great to meet the beavers, we think, but that's not likely to happen.

We paddle alongside grassy banks and weed-fringed wetland shores and admire emerging new leaves on salmonberry bushes. Blue herons rise vertically in front of us like helicopters, their enormous wings flapping as they gain just enough elevation to take them to another perch. As the sun rises higher, small western pond turtles clamber onto floating logs to spend the day warming themselves.

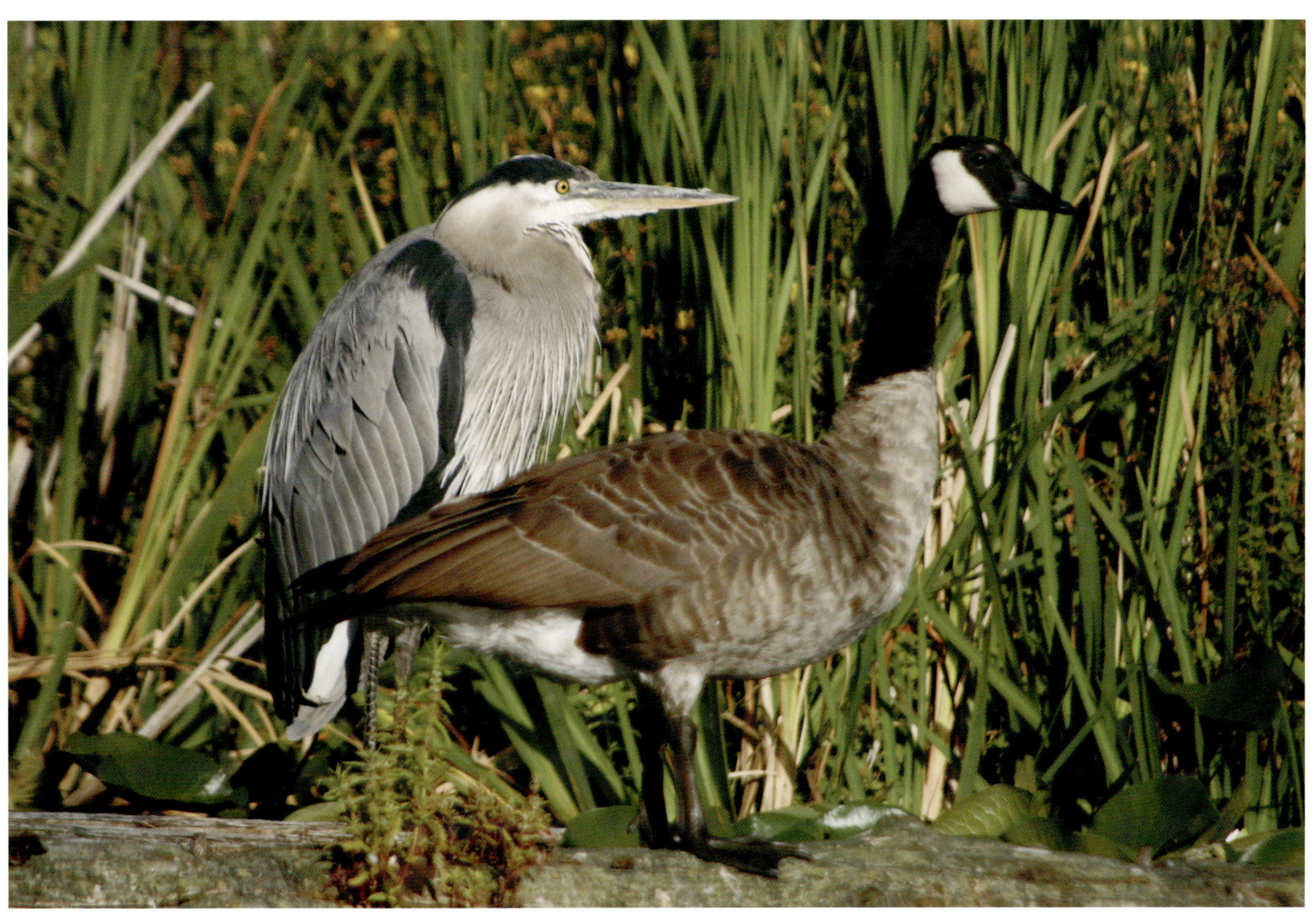

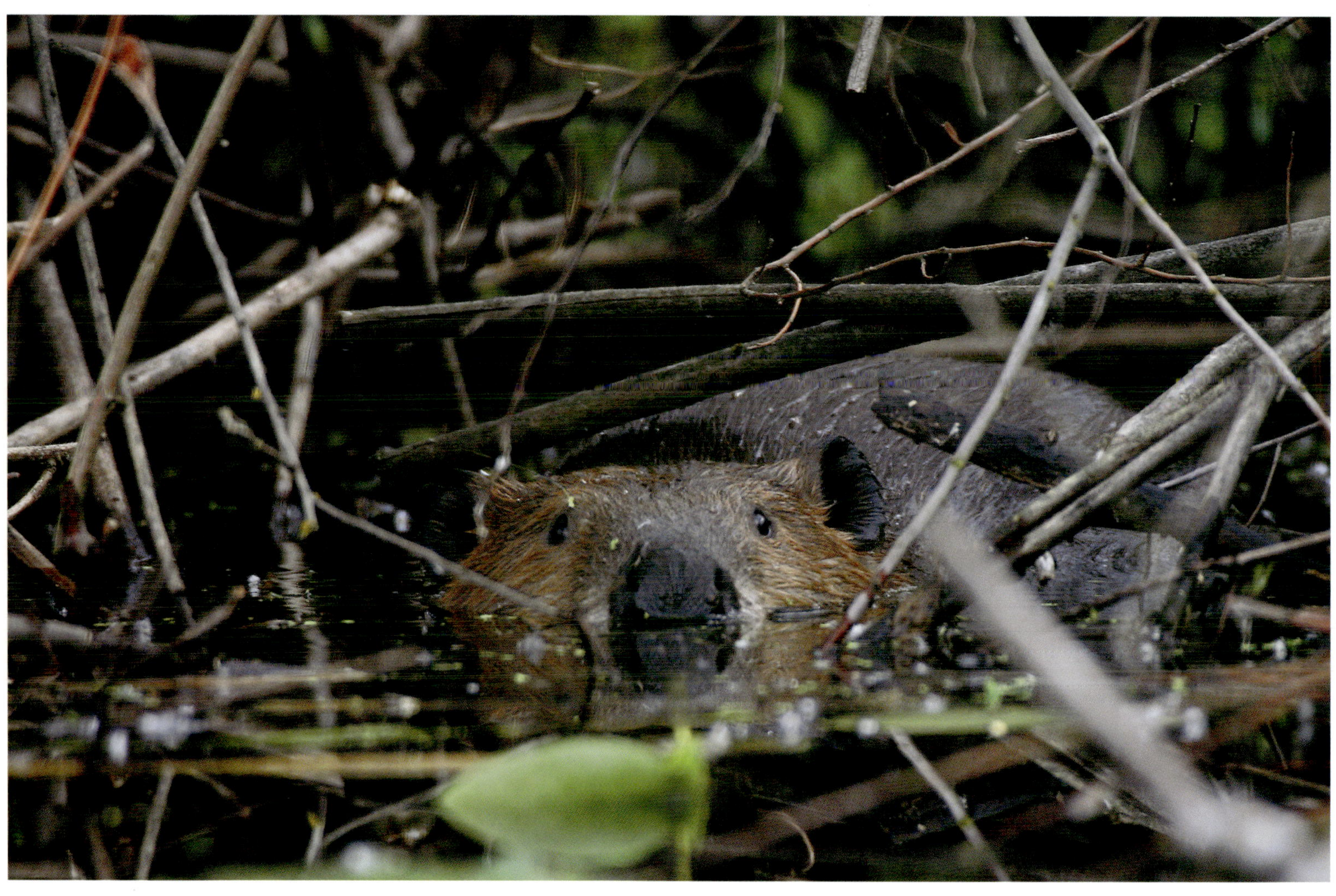

We duck our heads to paddle under a section of the freeway, briefly deafened by the roar directly overhead. Suddenly we spot movement in the bushes. Two small playful raccoons are wrestling and tumbling on a mossy level place. They pause to peer at us, one standing briefly on hind legs to check us out. Then they resume their silent play, one pulling on the ear of the other, while he rolls over to escape.

We paddle under another freeway bridge and come out into more open water, where pleasure-craft boat wakes will begin soon. As we look closely at the bufflehead and merganser ducks approaching us, one of the heads seems different. It has no bill, and this bird has small ears. It's the beaver himself, swimming directly toward us. Sure that he will dive at any moment, we stow our paddles and gaze at the small vigorous swimmer. Undeterred, he comes right alongside the canoe and then continues on, perhaps searching for new sticks and branches to chew.

The incongruity of wildlife coexisting and flourishing alongside the freeway continues to amaze us.

— *Joan Burton*

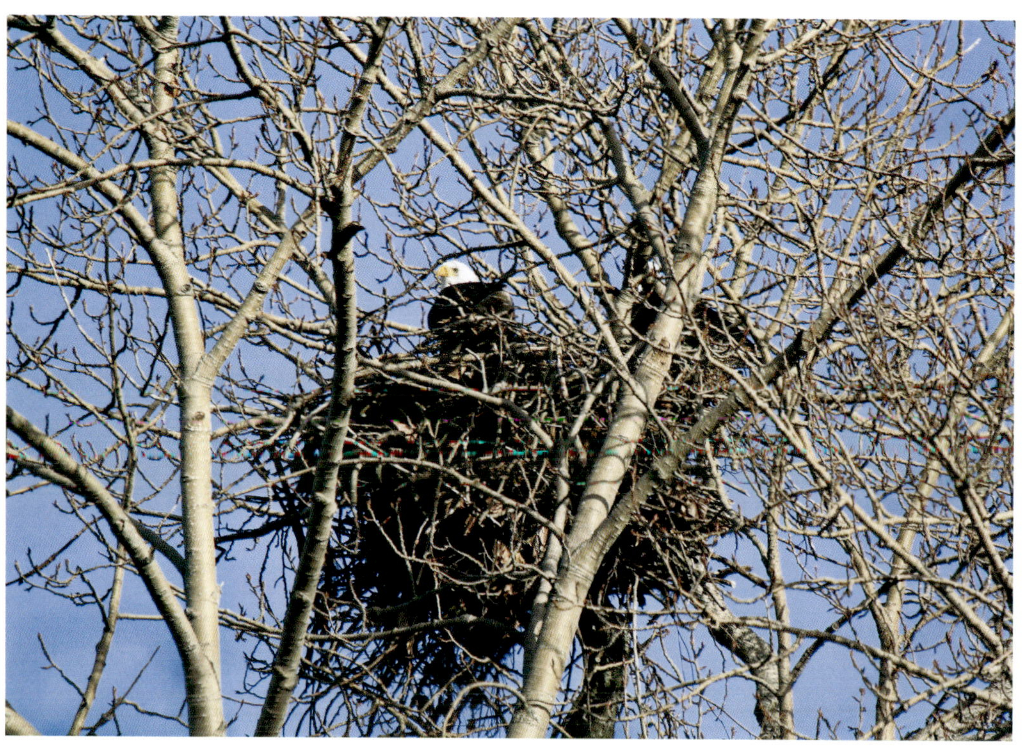

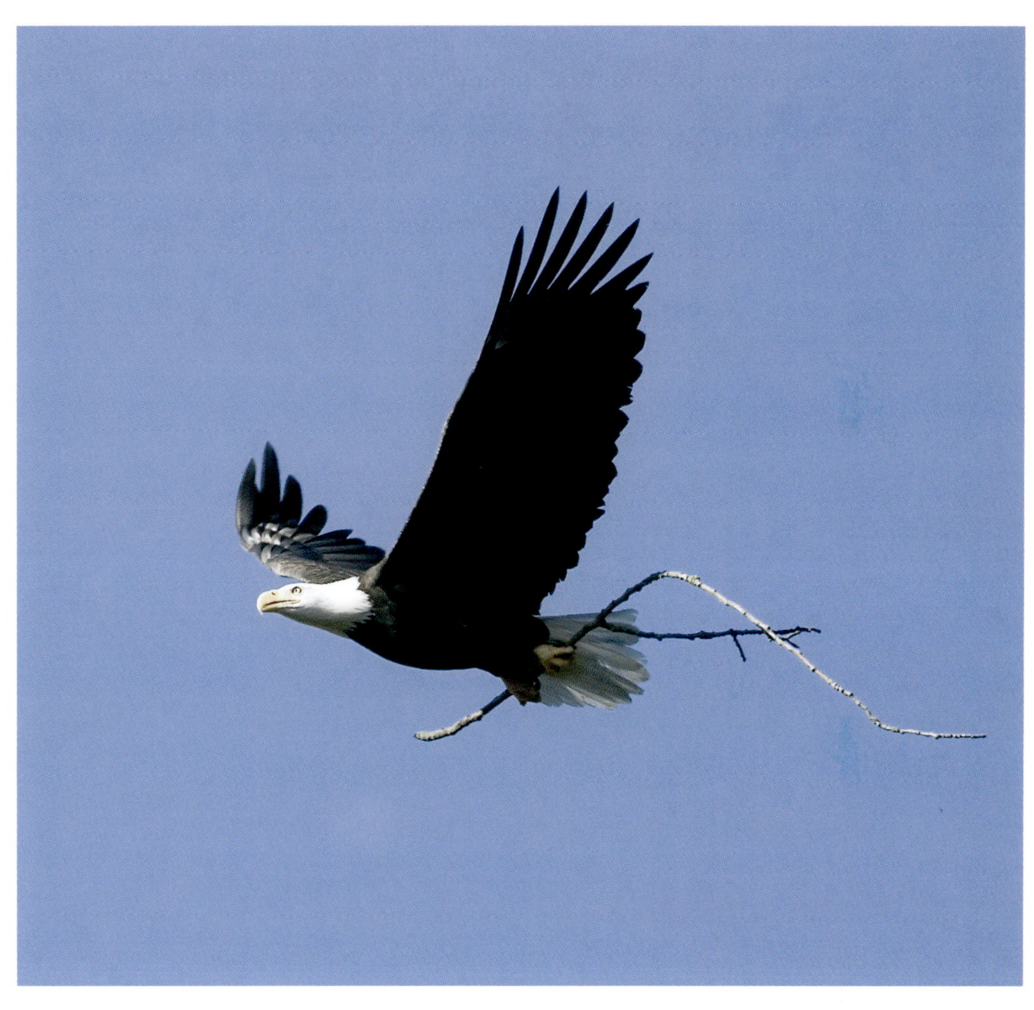

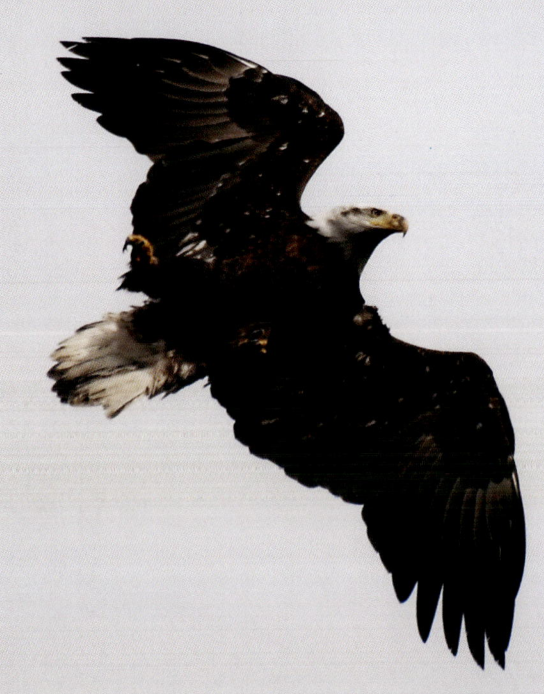

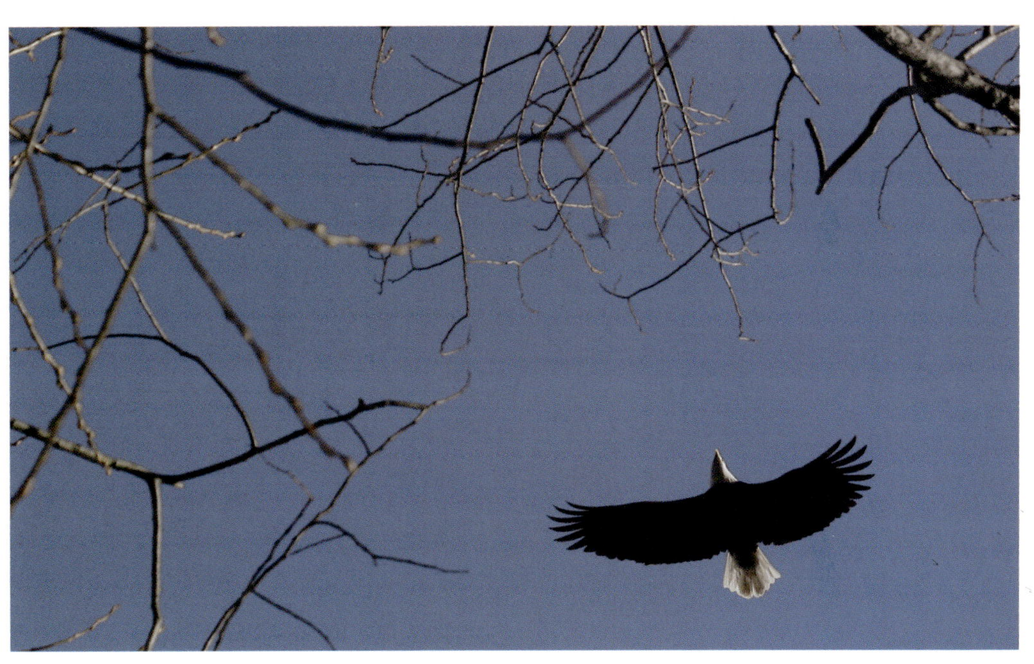

Birds' songs serenade.
Breezes rustle through tall reeds.
Eagles scream on high.

— haiku by Marcia M. Mueller

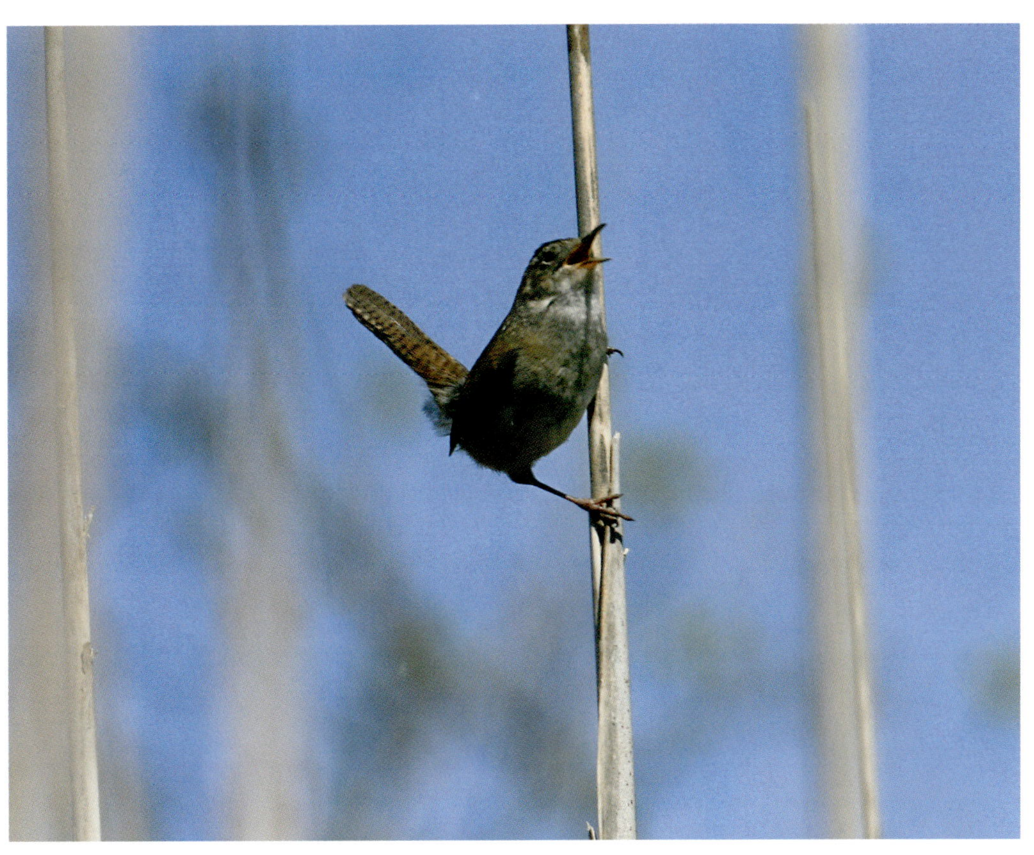

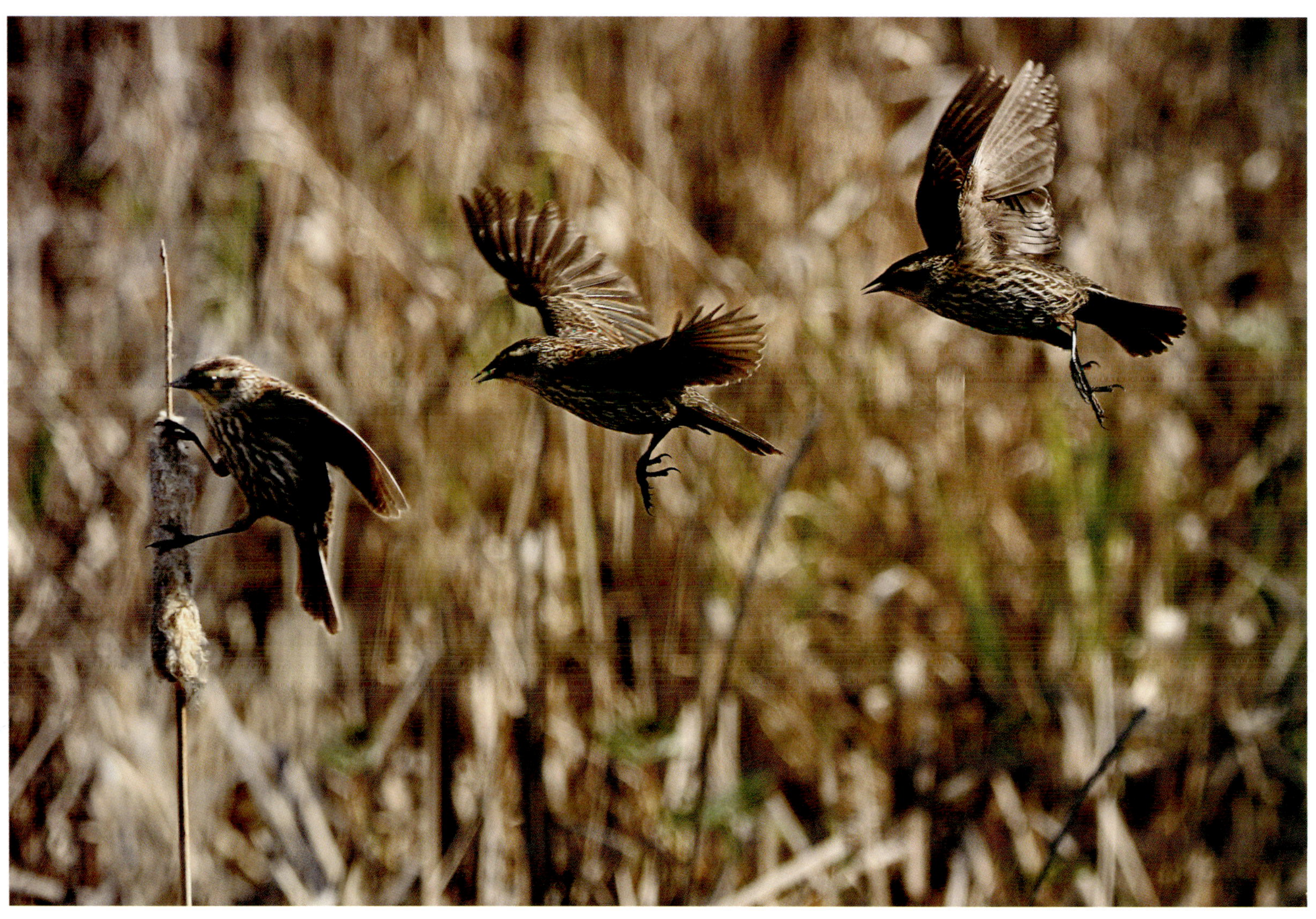

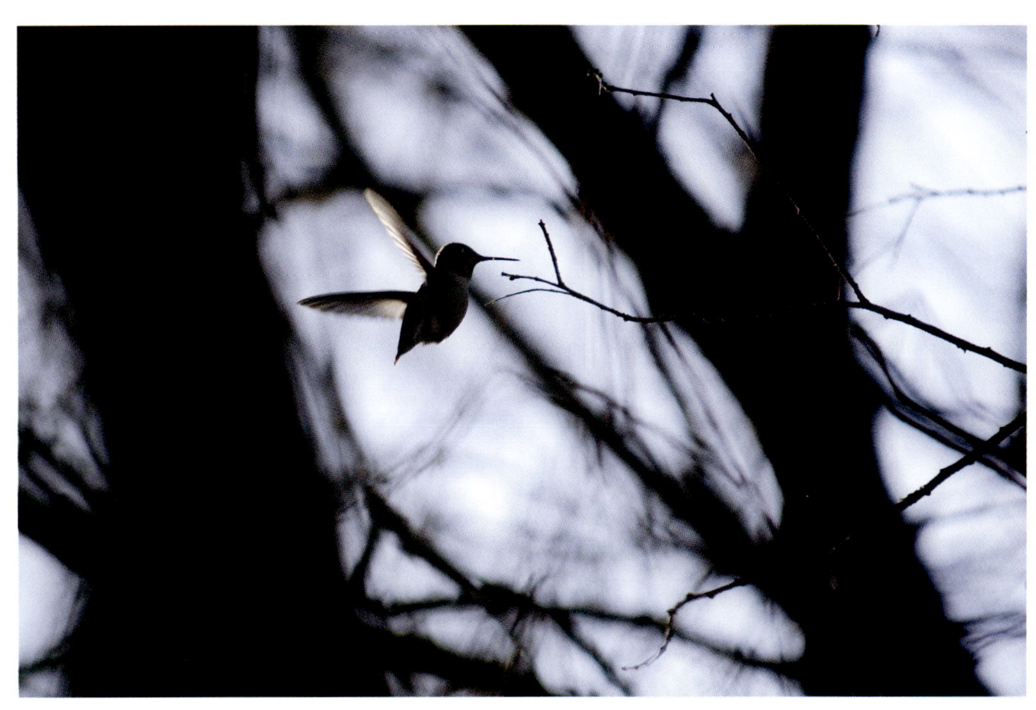

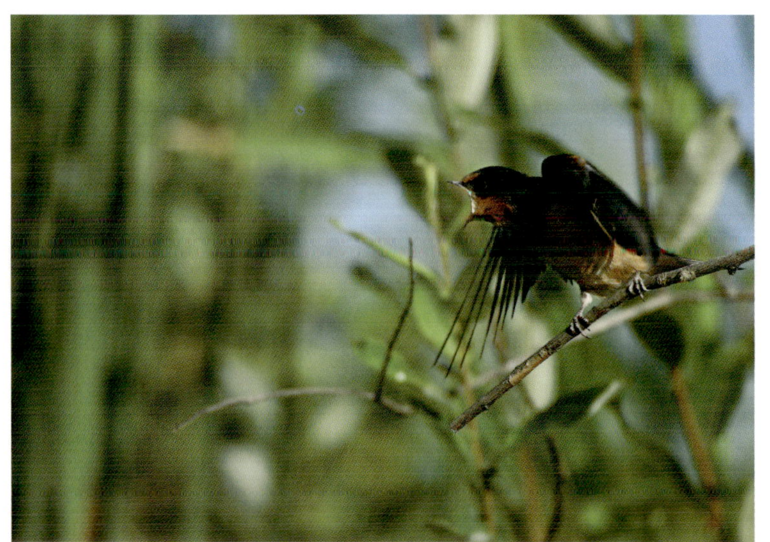

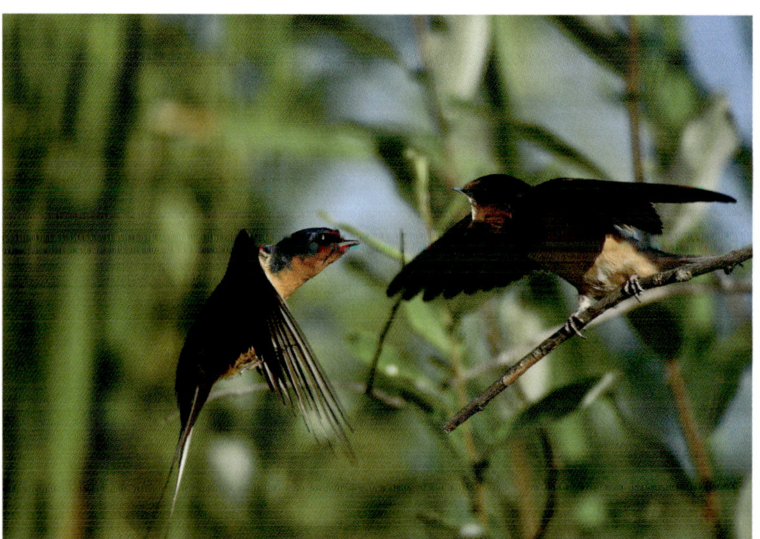

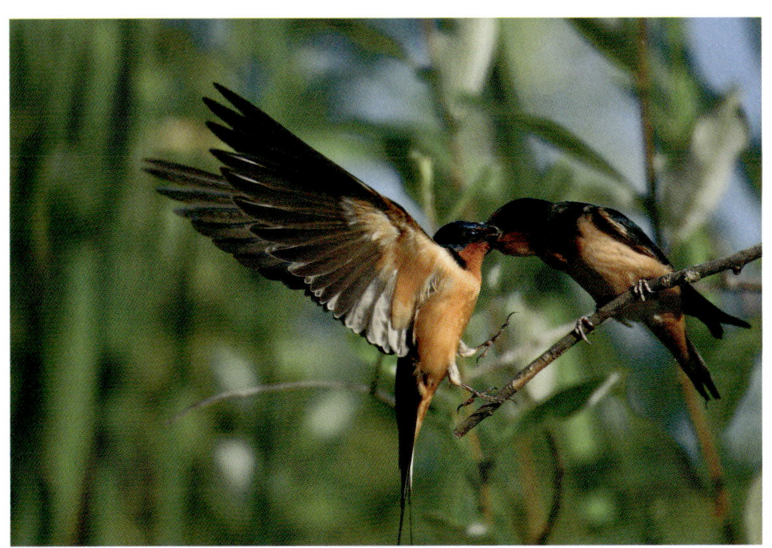

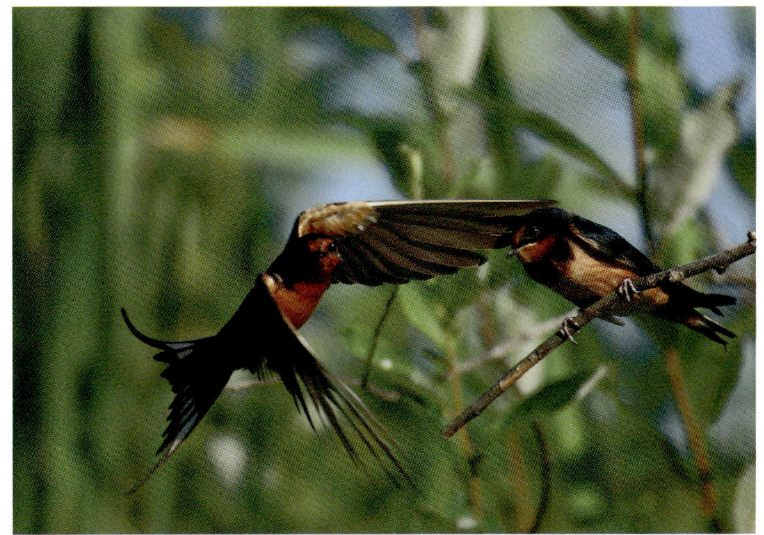

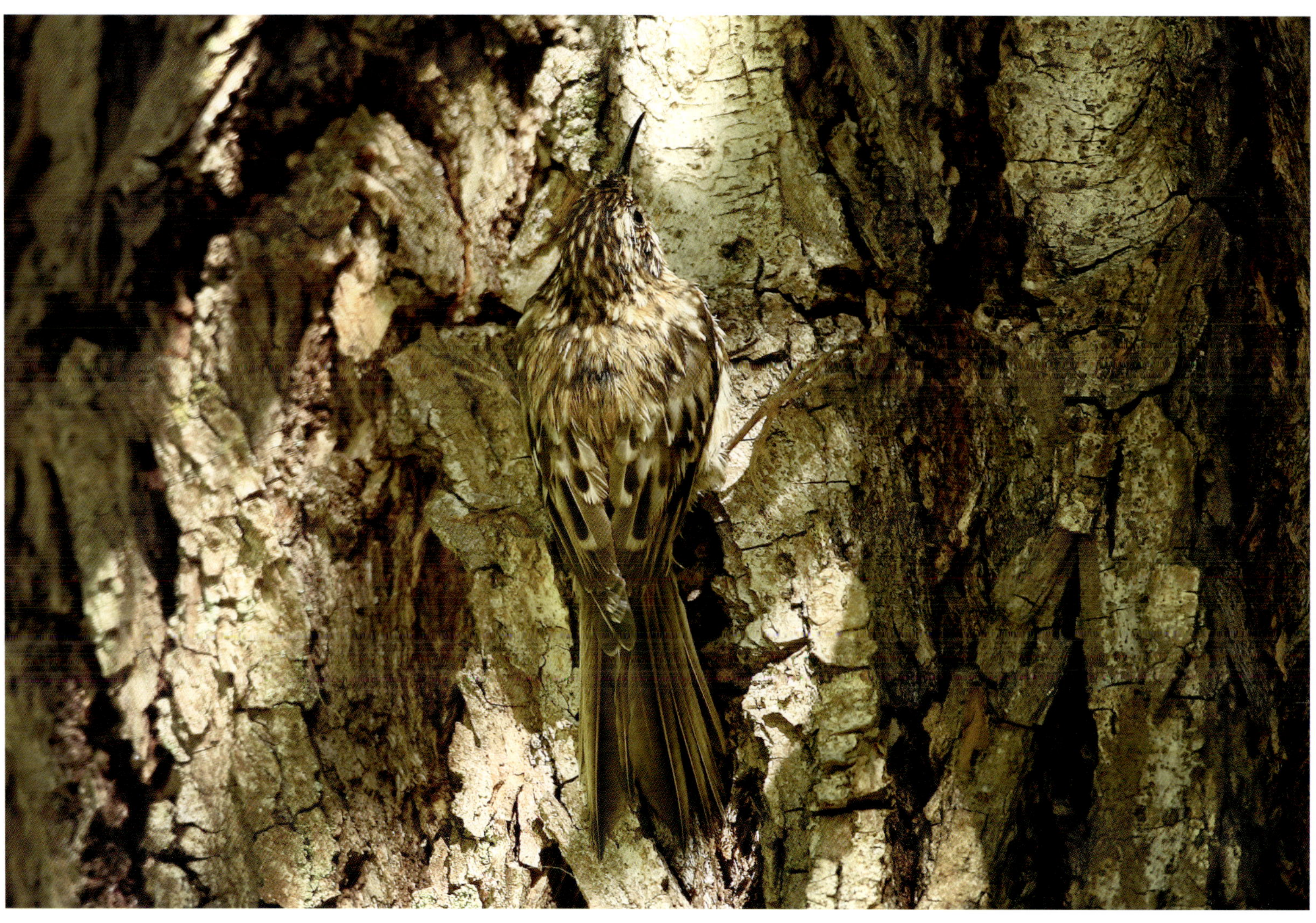

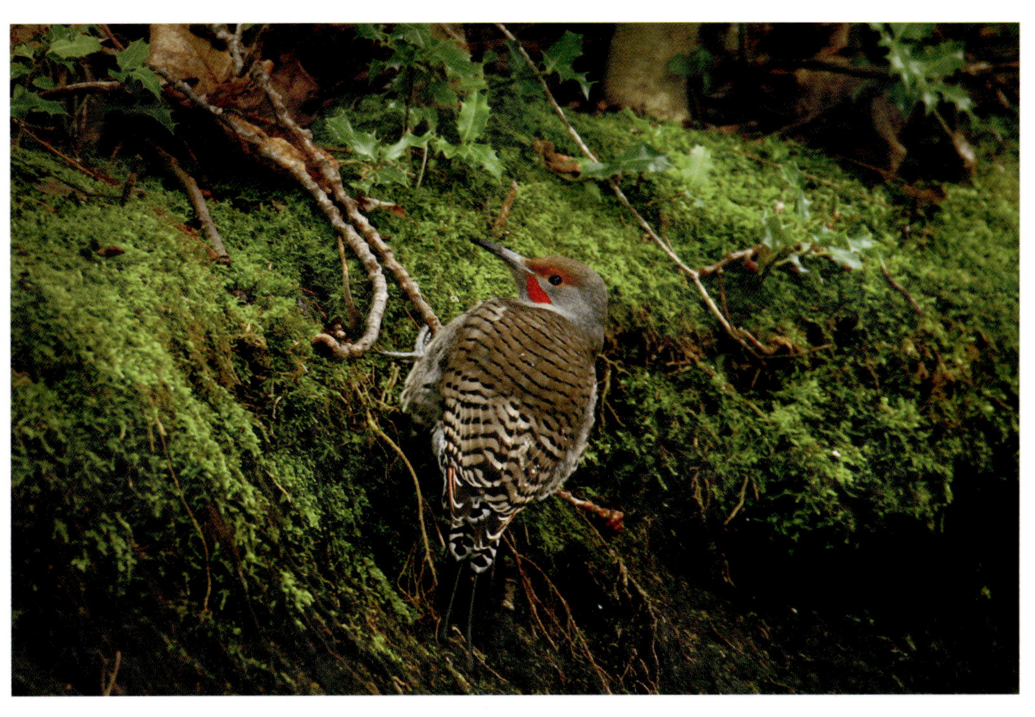

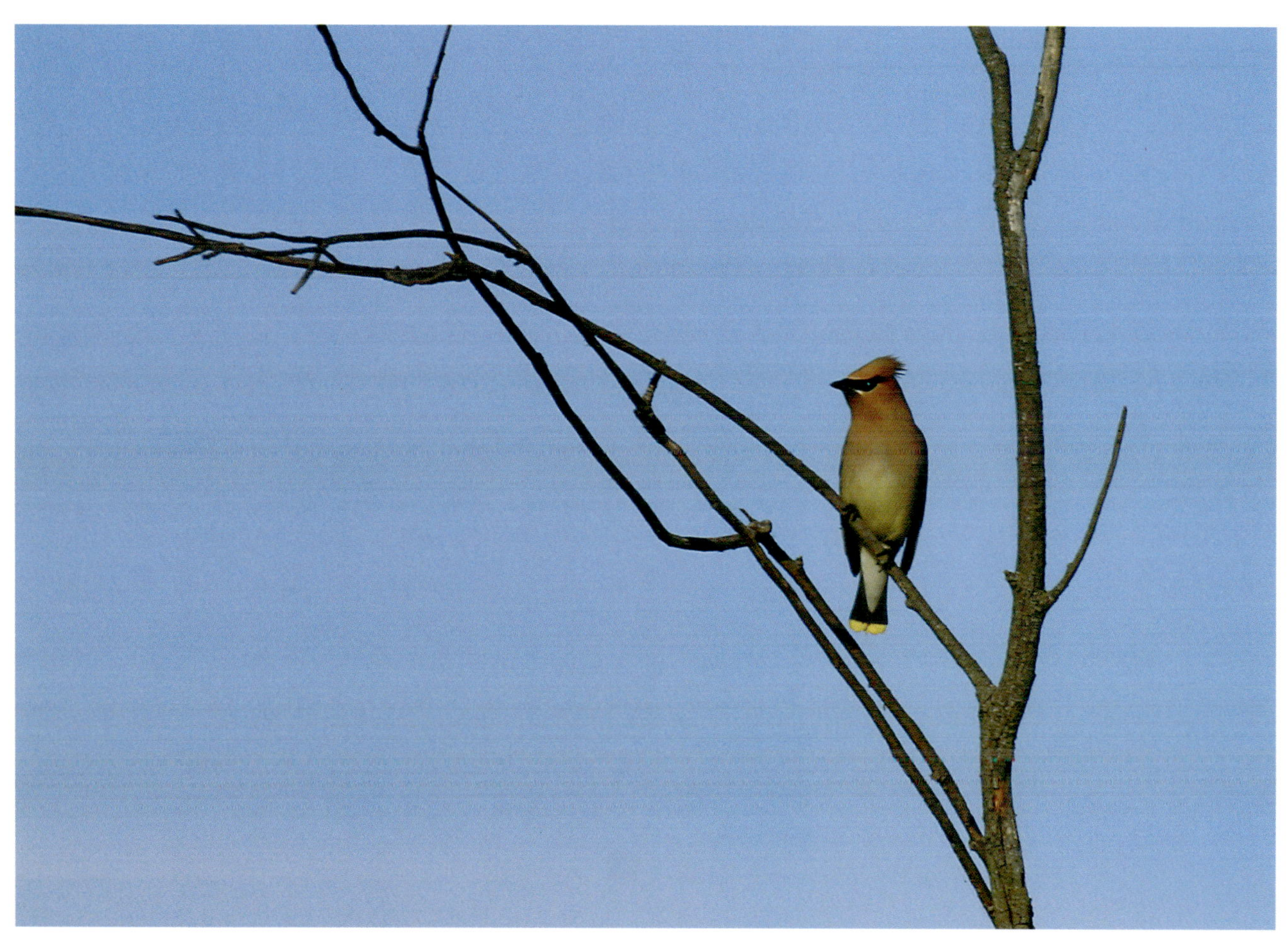

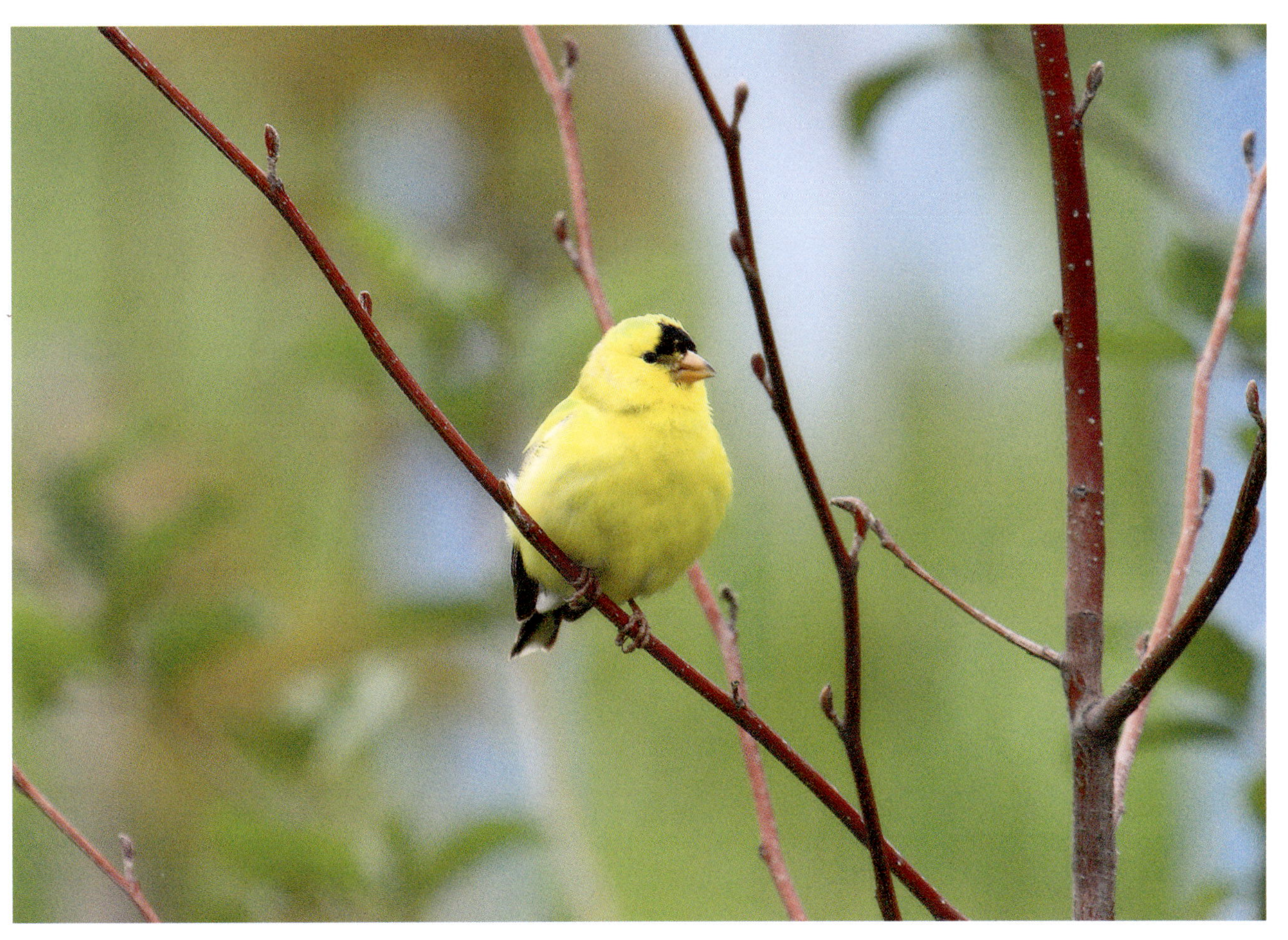

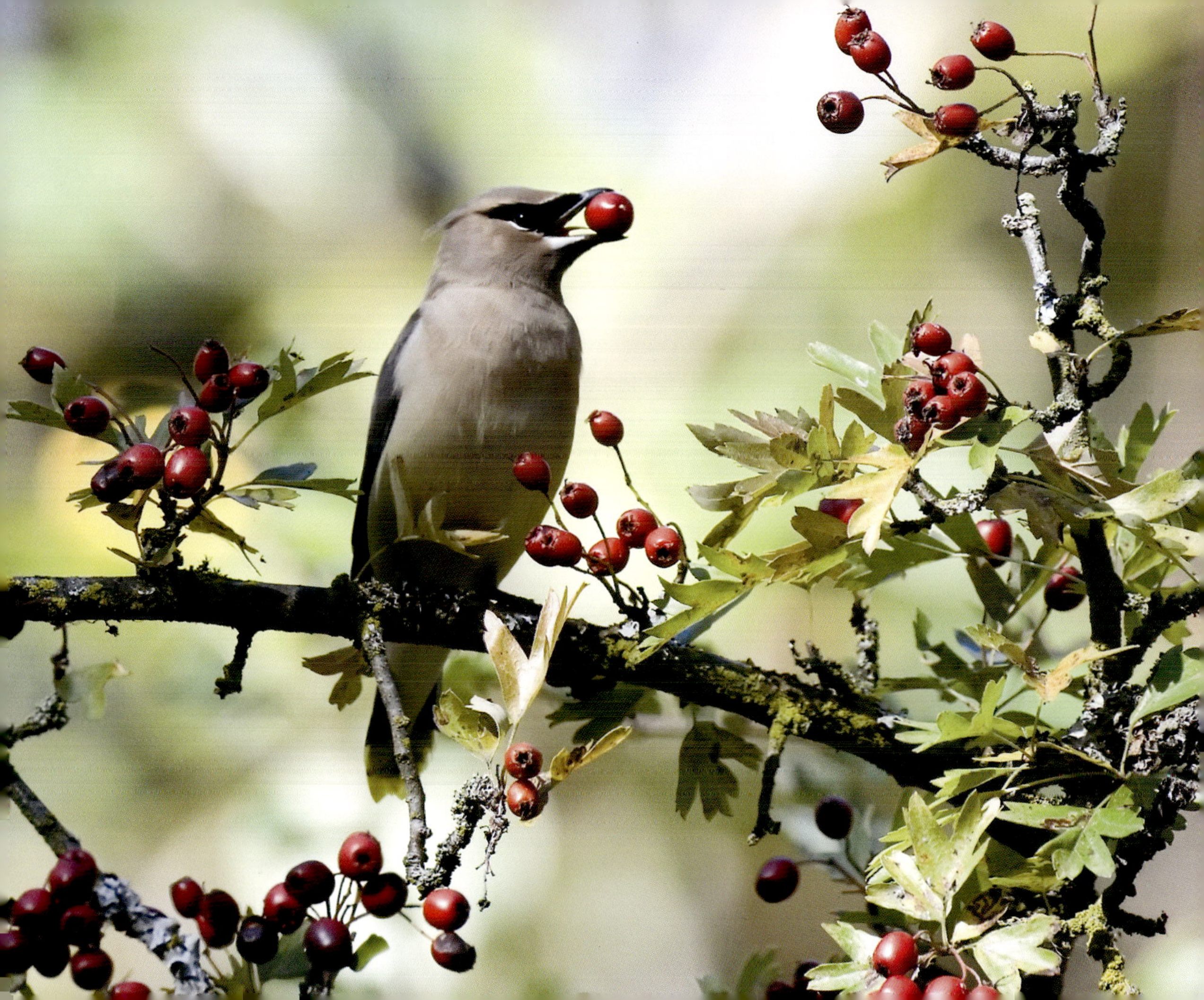

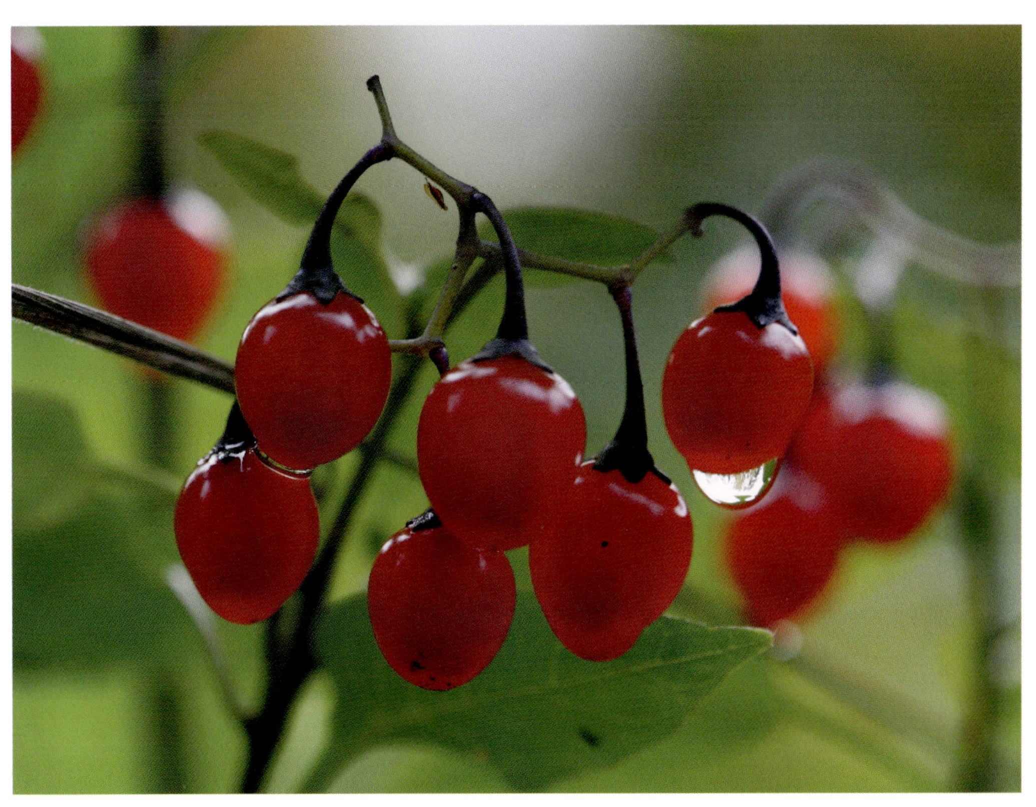

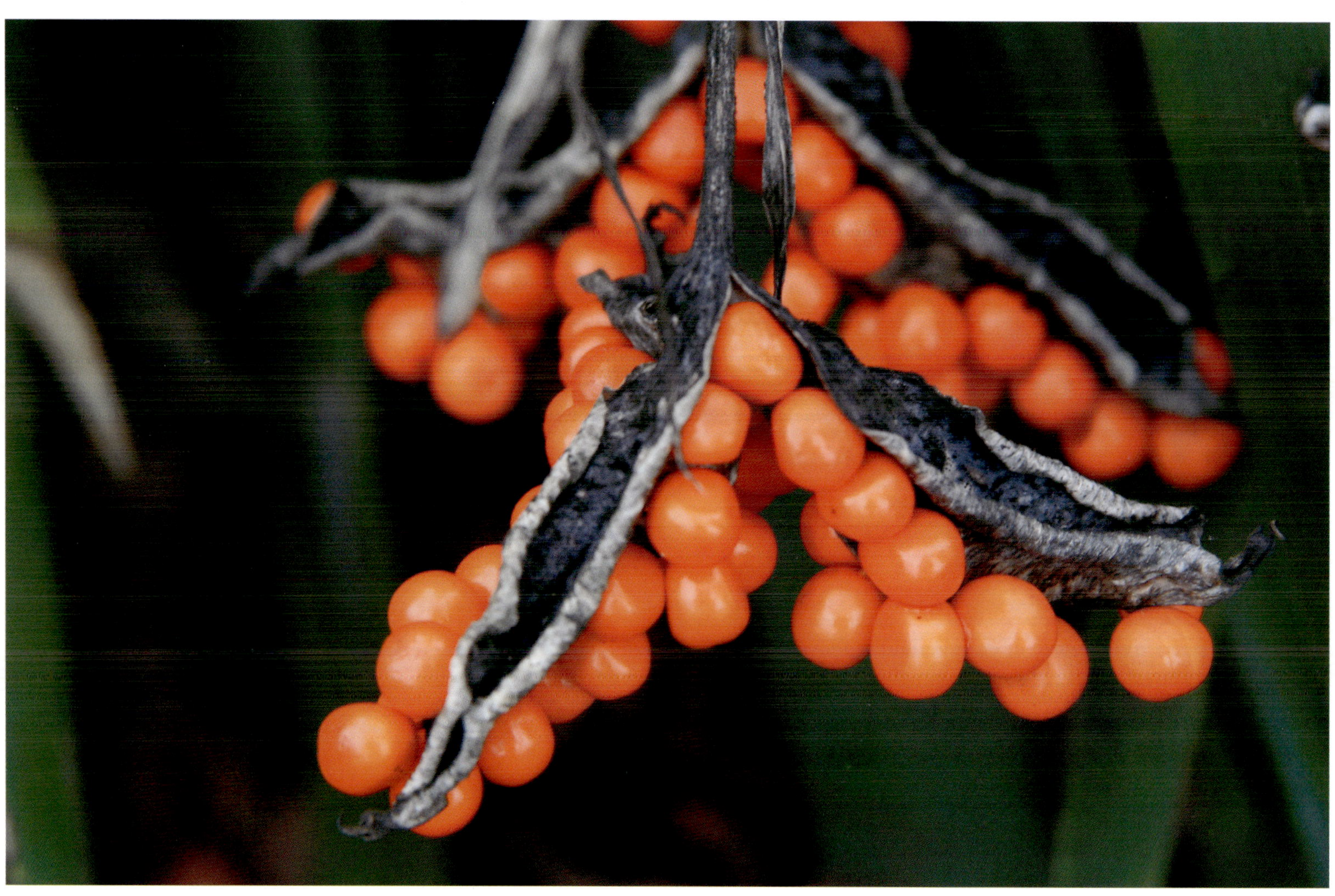

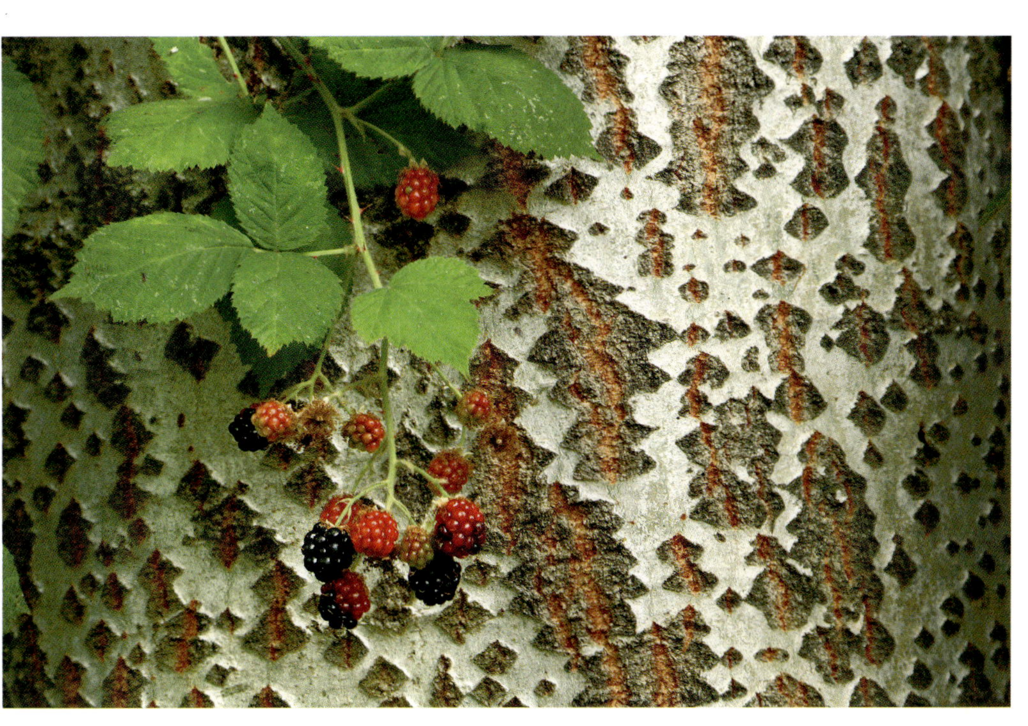

Before European settlement, abundant wetlands graced the ravines and lakeshore around what is now Union Bay with an energetic solitude. From hillside seeps luminous with skunk cabbage through lush fern-lined ravines to vast tule marshes resonating with red-winged blackbird calls, water from winter rains meandered over land and through the soil, unimpeded by buildings, unhurried by drains. What remains of these wetlands still has the power to command studied silence, even in their diminishment.

Absorbed in our reverie with the wings of a blue dasher, we can be forgiven for assuming that the willow swamps, water lily fields, and cattail marshes that compose the largest wetland complex in Seattle are, too, relicts from the past. In reality this verdant arc around the western edges of Union Bay is less than 100 years old, a mere infant learning to speak in ecological time. When the construction of the Lake Washington Ship Canal in 1916 lowered the lake by 11 feet, fertile lake-bed sediments were exposed to the sun and air to be colonized by wind-, water-, and bird-borne seeds. A wetland was born.

What has persisted of this terra nova through decades of urban development lies protected within two parts of the University of Washington Botanic Gardens: the Washington Park Arboretum and the Union Bay Natural Area. This young ecosystem has been, and will be, nurtured toward maturity by generations of caretakers from the university, city, and surrounding community. Invading Himalayan blackberry and bittersweet nightshade will be replaced by Pacific willow and red-twig dogwood. Western red cedars and western hemlocks will rise up through black cottonwood and red alder that have come to the end of their time. With purple loosestrife suppressed, pied-billed grebes will nest as they once did among the tule. We hope that hundreds of years hence someone, finding their attention calmly tracing the flight of a heron, will feel the cool shade of the evergreen canopy above and assume that this wildness has always been there waiting for them—in one sense it will have been.

— Rodney Pond

University of Washington Botanic Gardens

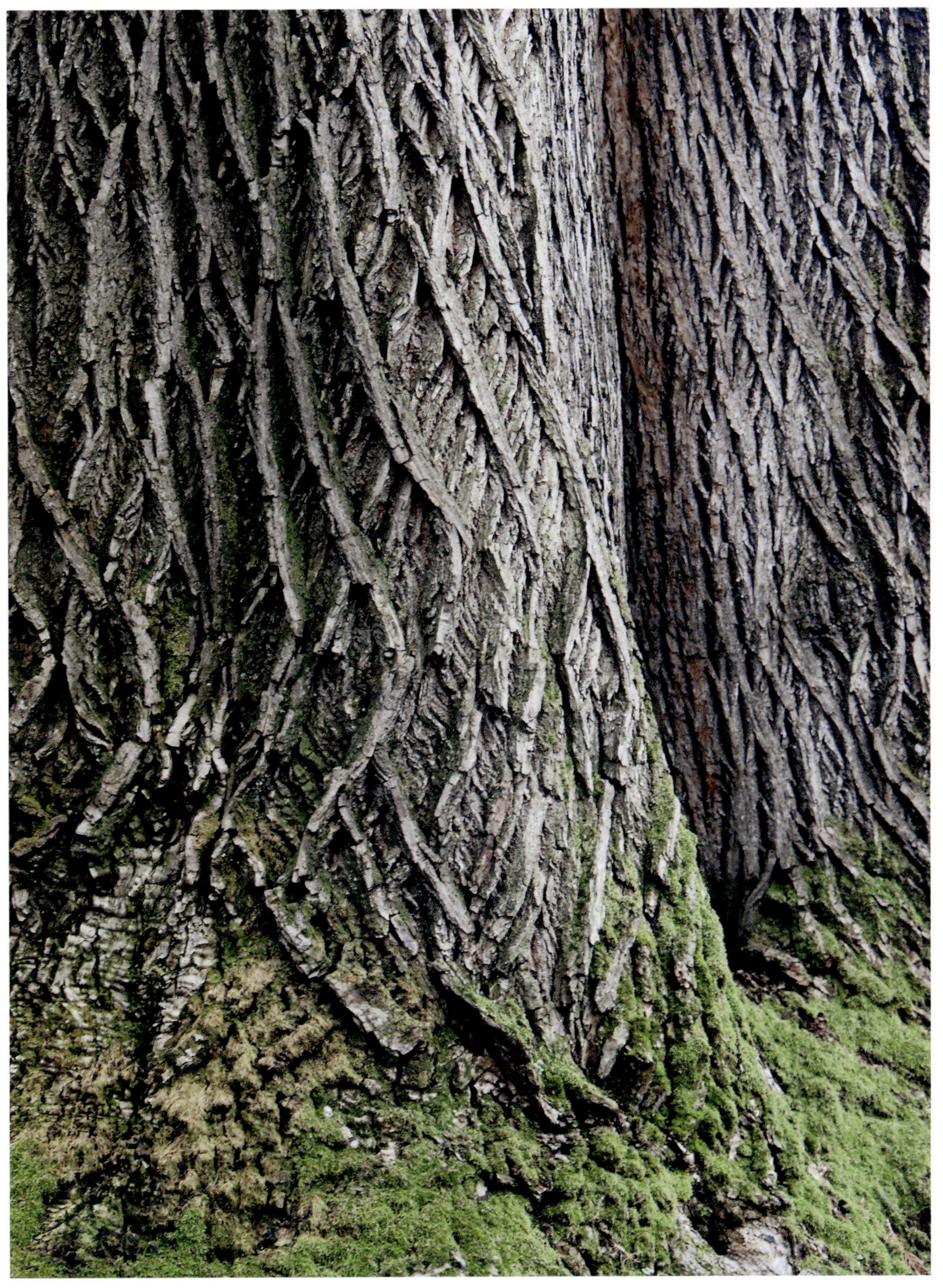

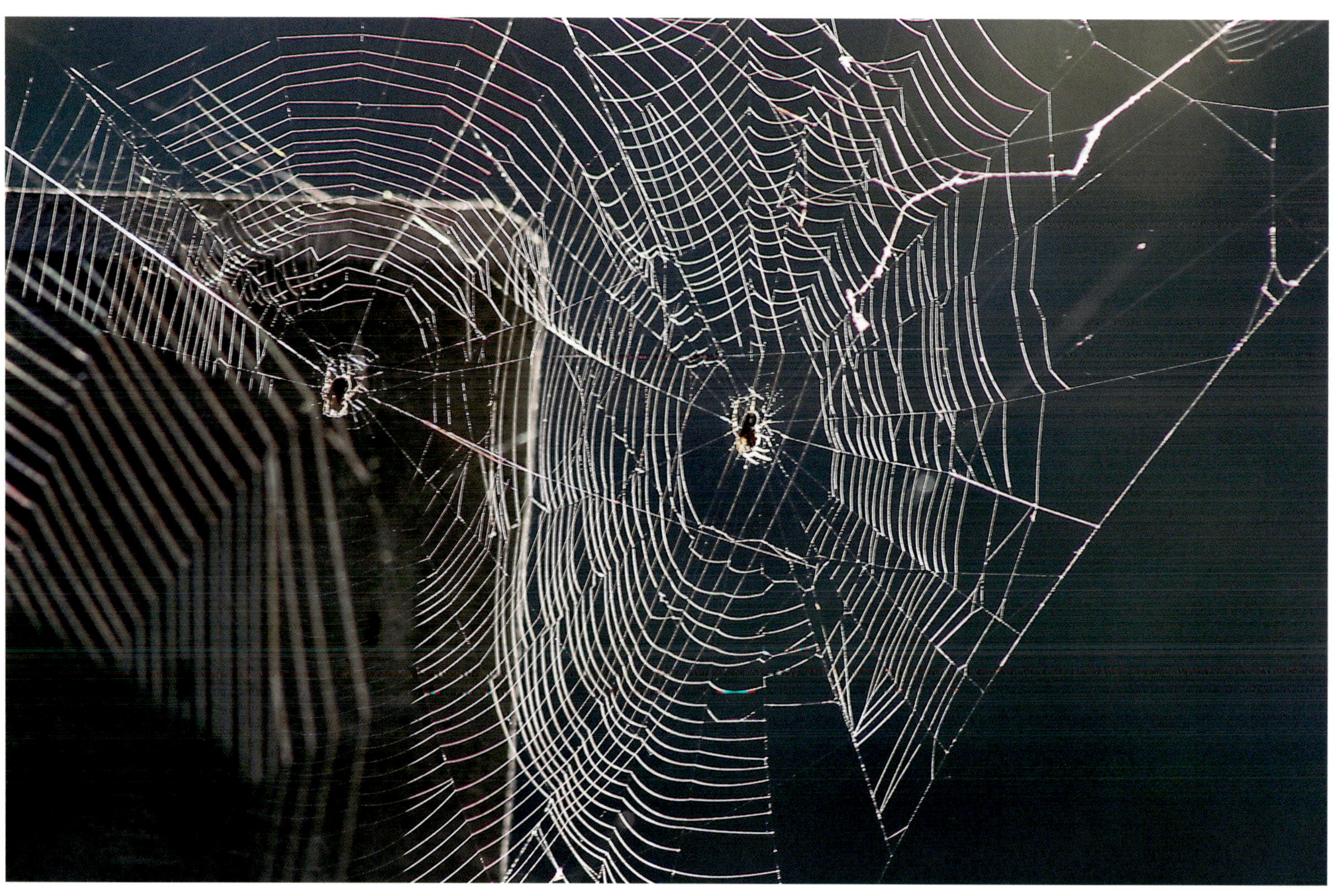

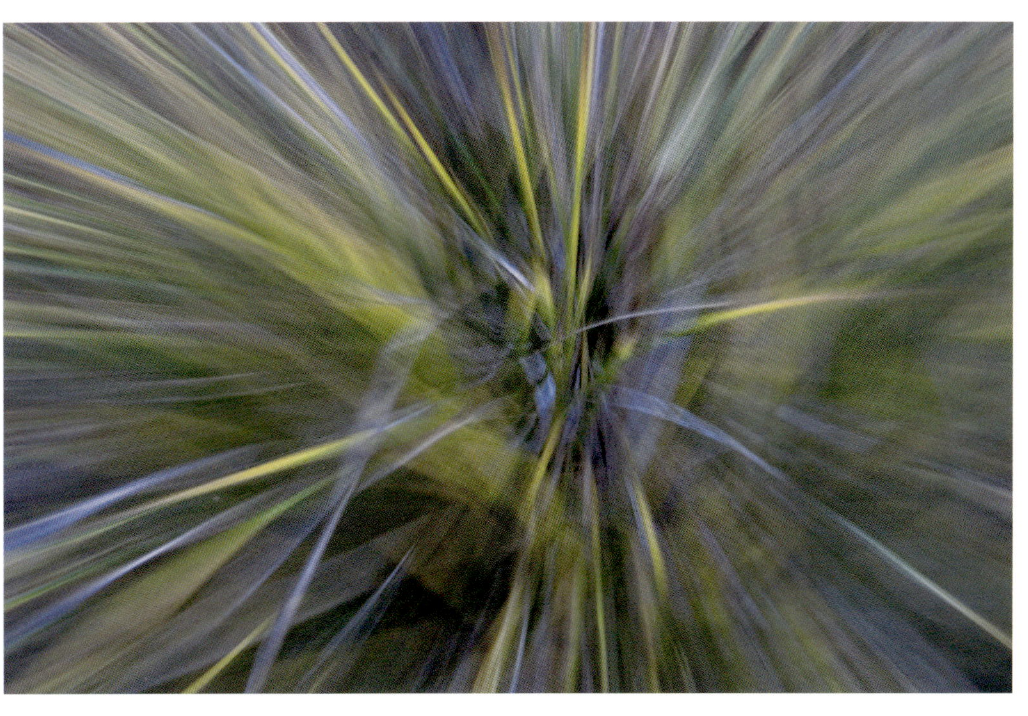

Humans have a strong and essential bond with nature. We are fortunate in the Northwest to have wilderness and shoreline, mountains and prairies, all within an easy day's trip. But many of our citizens, particularly the young, seldom leave our city limits.

Fortunately, farsighted leaders of Seattle and the University of Washington joined to create a remarkable natural area in the center of a great city. It is a spiritual experience to walk among the wetlands and the upland forests. Children see, with greater clarity than adults, the simple interactions of plants and animals within the framework of complex ecosystems.

I have vivid memories of visiting the Arboretum with my parents as a child, marveling at the variety and magnitude of this special place. It gave me my first taste of nature long before I discovered the wilderness of the Olympic Mountains. Nancy and I now see the same wonderment and growing love of nature as we traipse with our grandchildren through the wetlands of the Arboretum.

My generation is blessed with the wisdom of past generations. They preserved great national parks during a generation of nation building. Washington State preserved natural shorelines and unique open spaces. Our city leaders created the Arboretum we enjoy today. Our generation must be as wise and protective in creating a natural legacy for our grandchildren.

Seattle has been discovered, and as our population surges, it is imperative to protect every inch of natural shoreline, every bog of unique wetlands, and every grove of special trees. Once we lose our natural heritage, it can never be regained. We who have enjoyed the Arboretum and its unique treasures have a special responsibility to preserve them for future generations.

— Governor Dan Evans

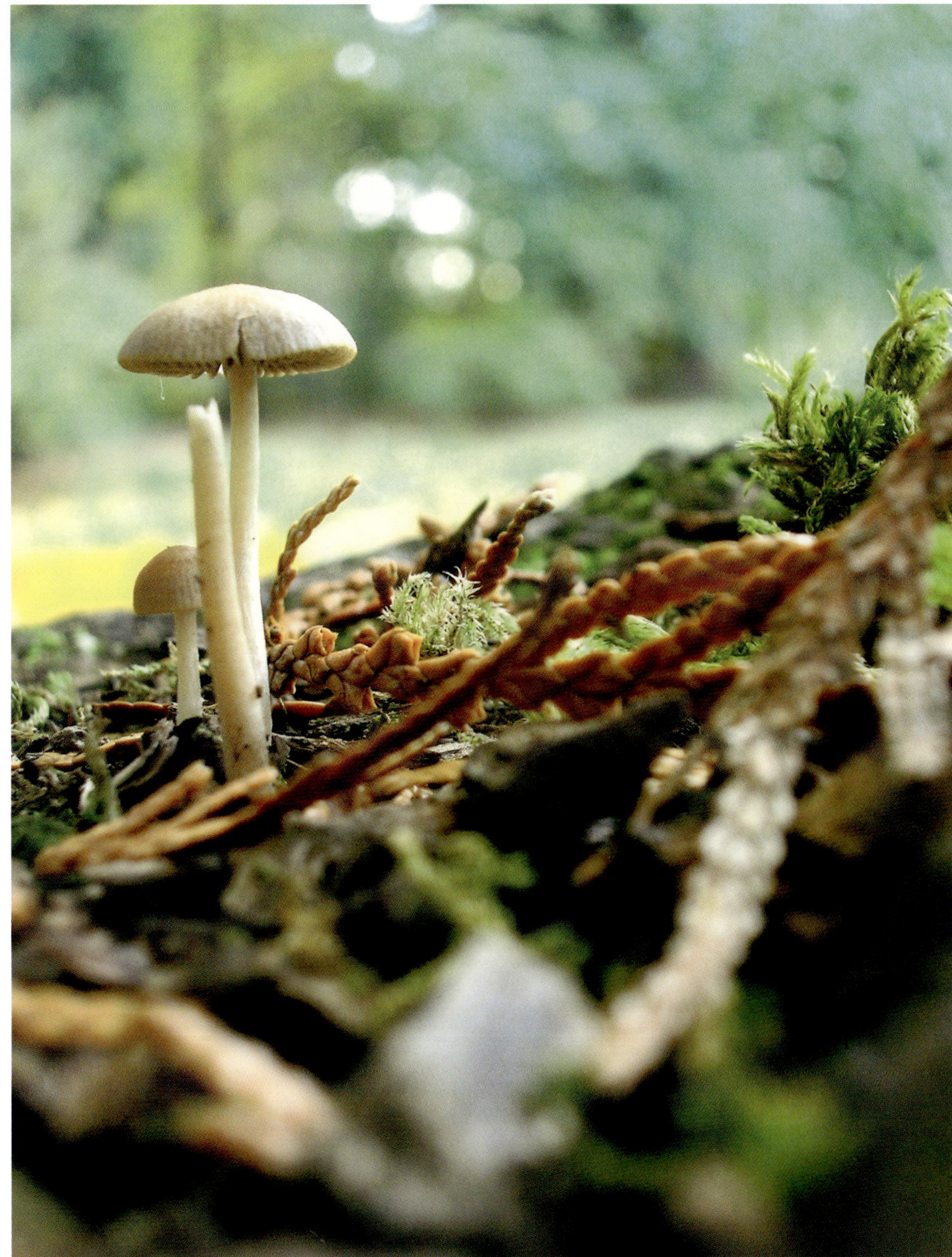

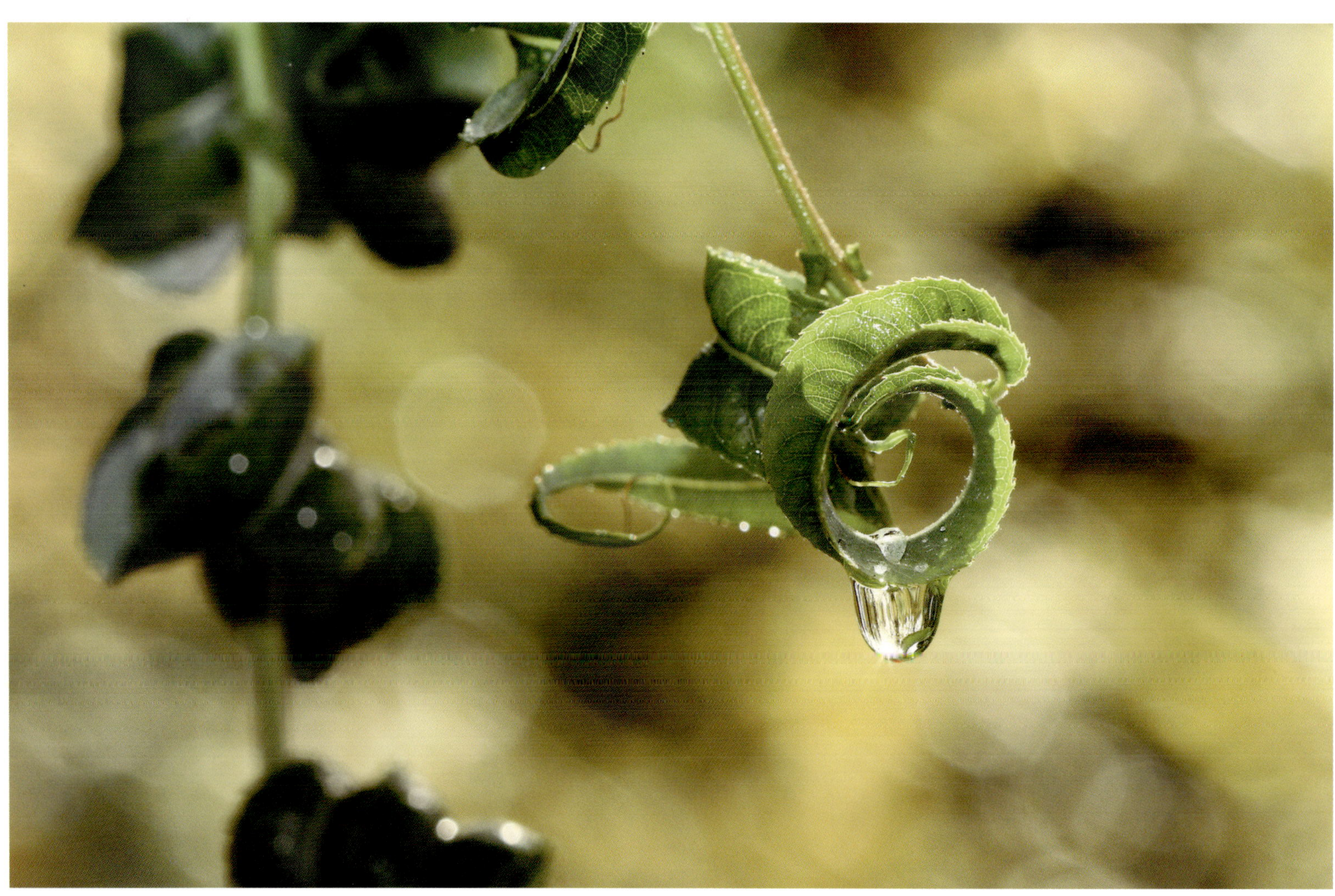

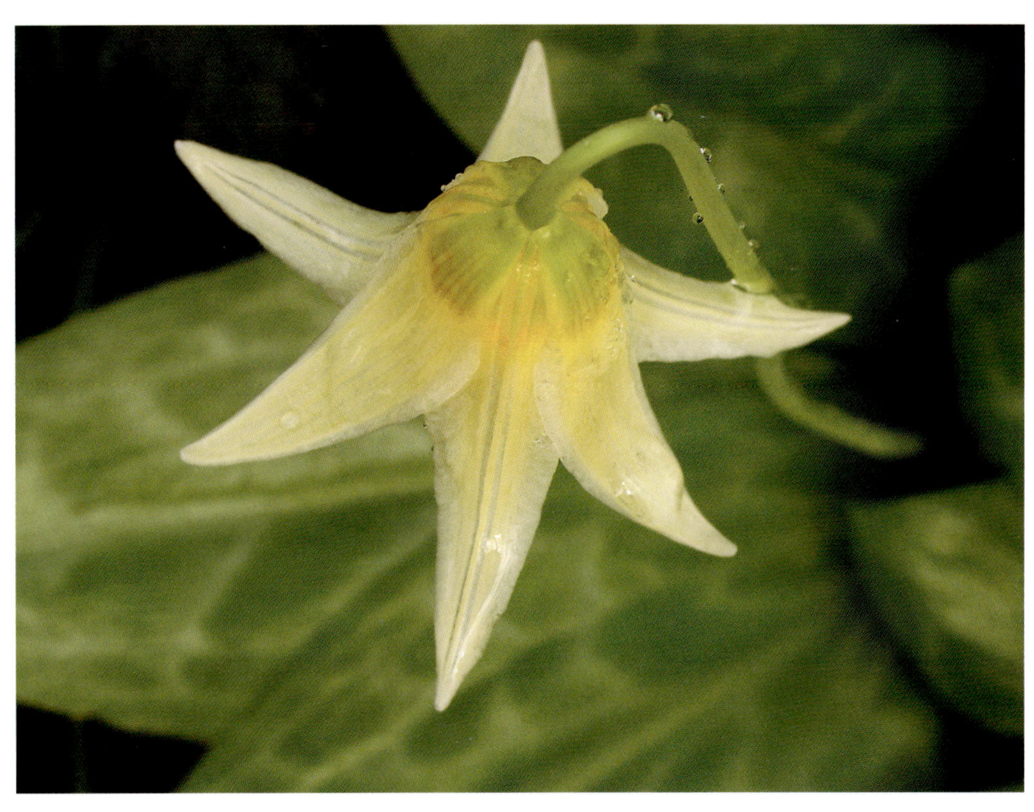

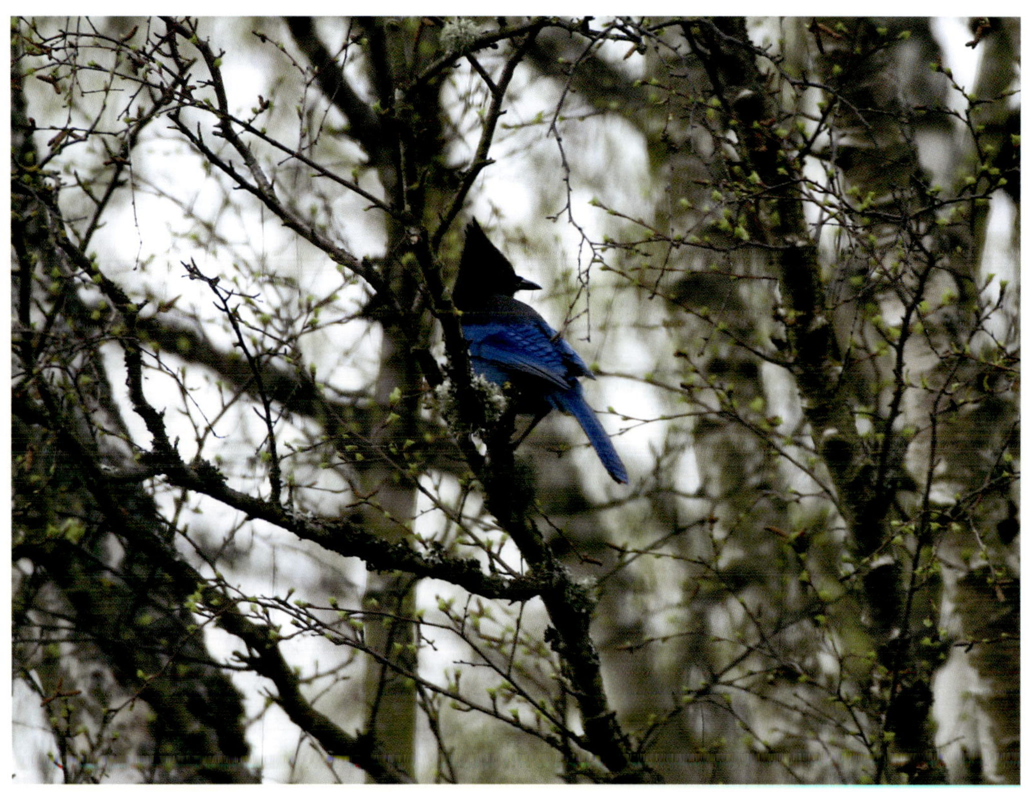

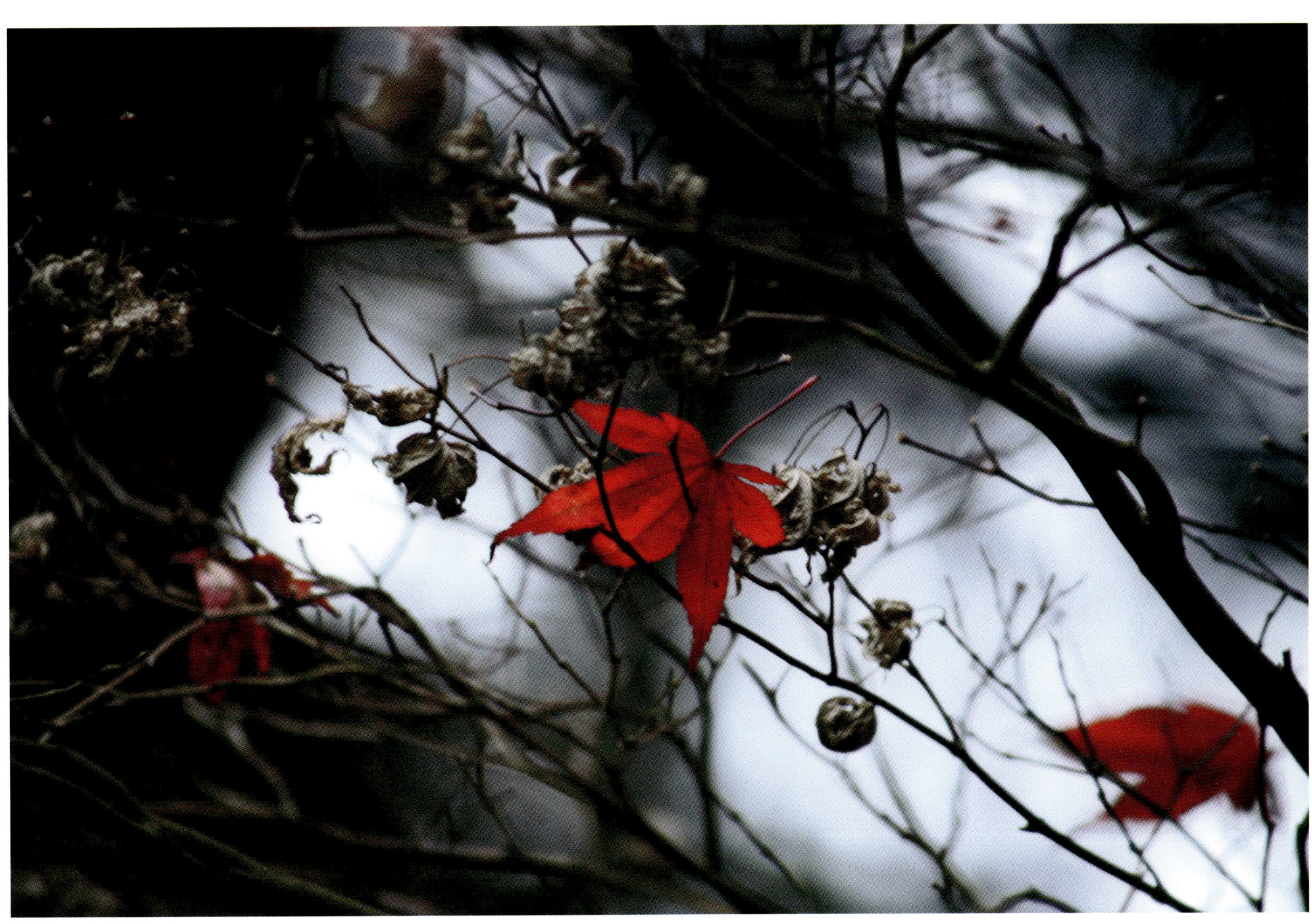

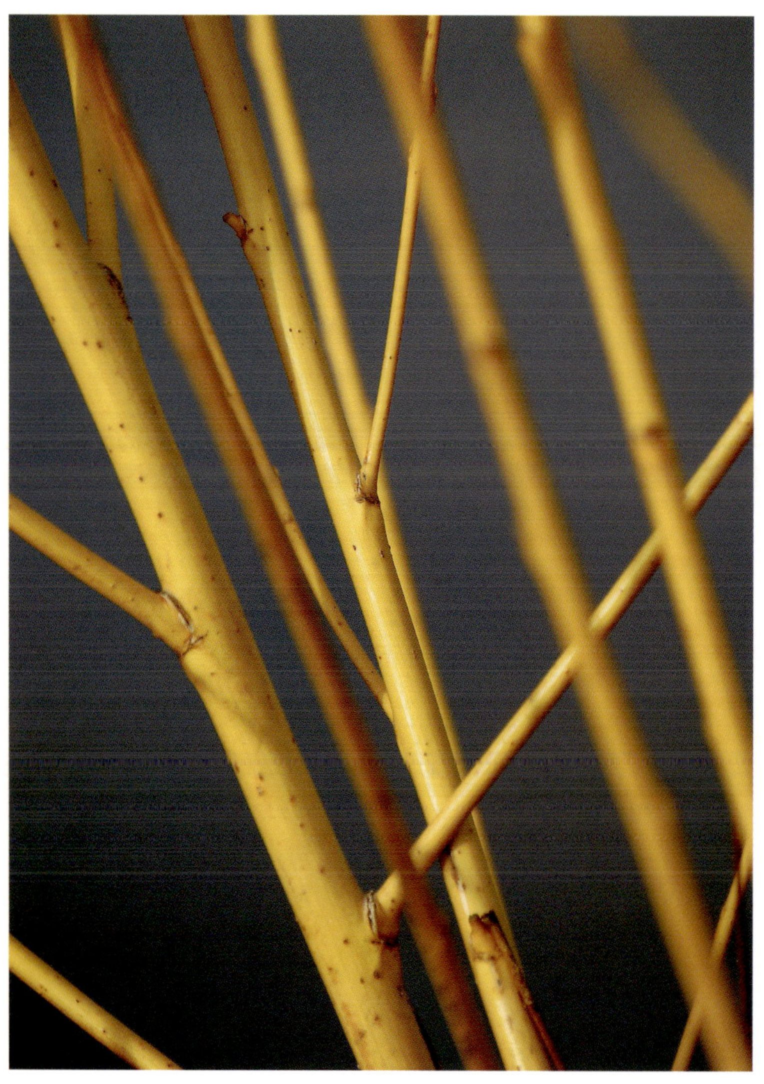

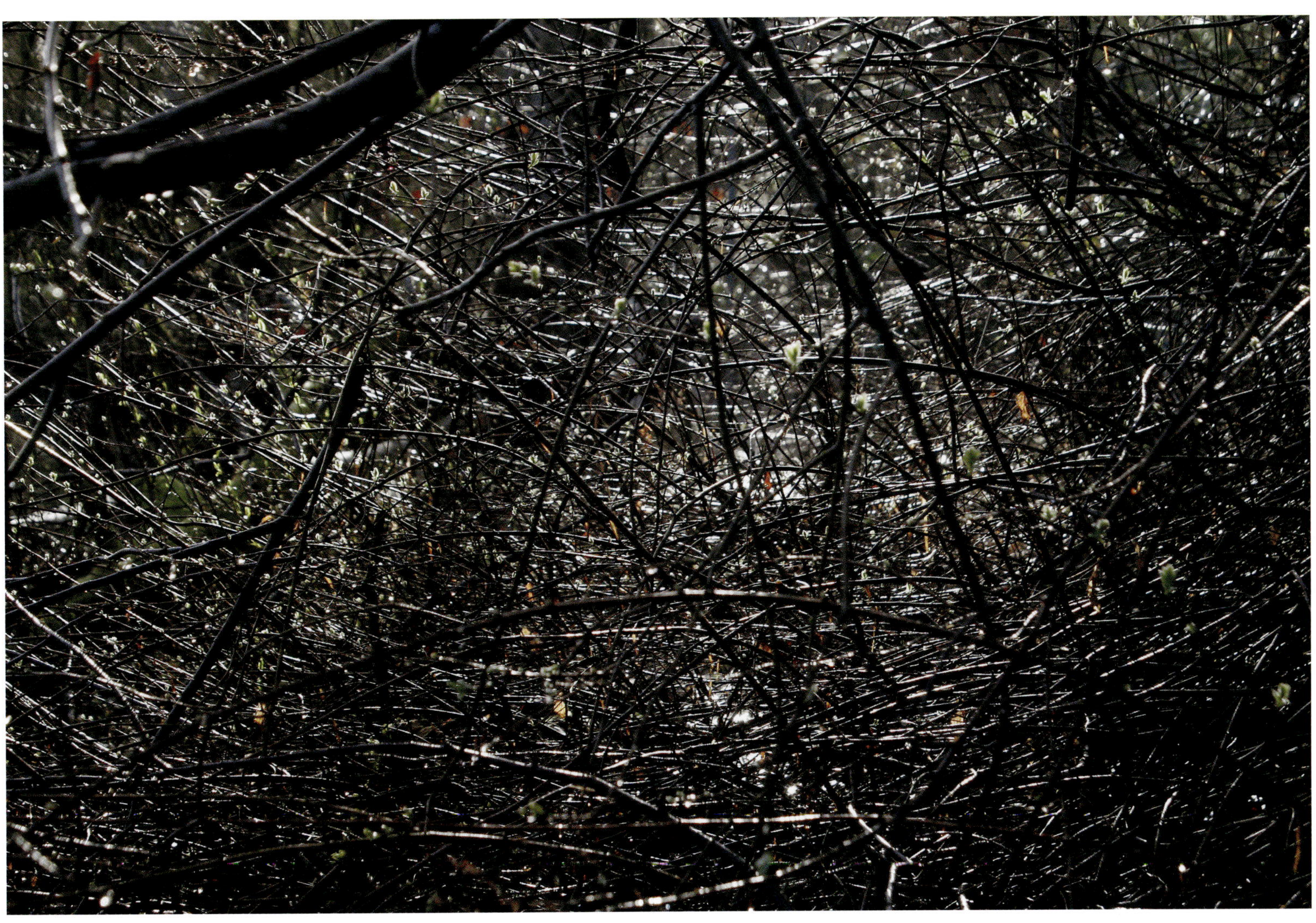

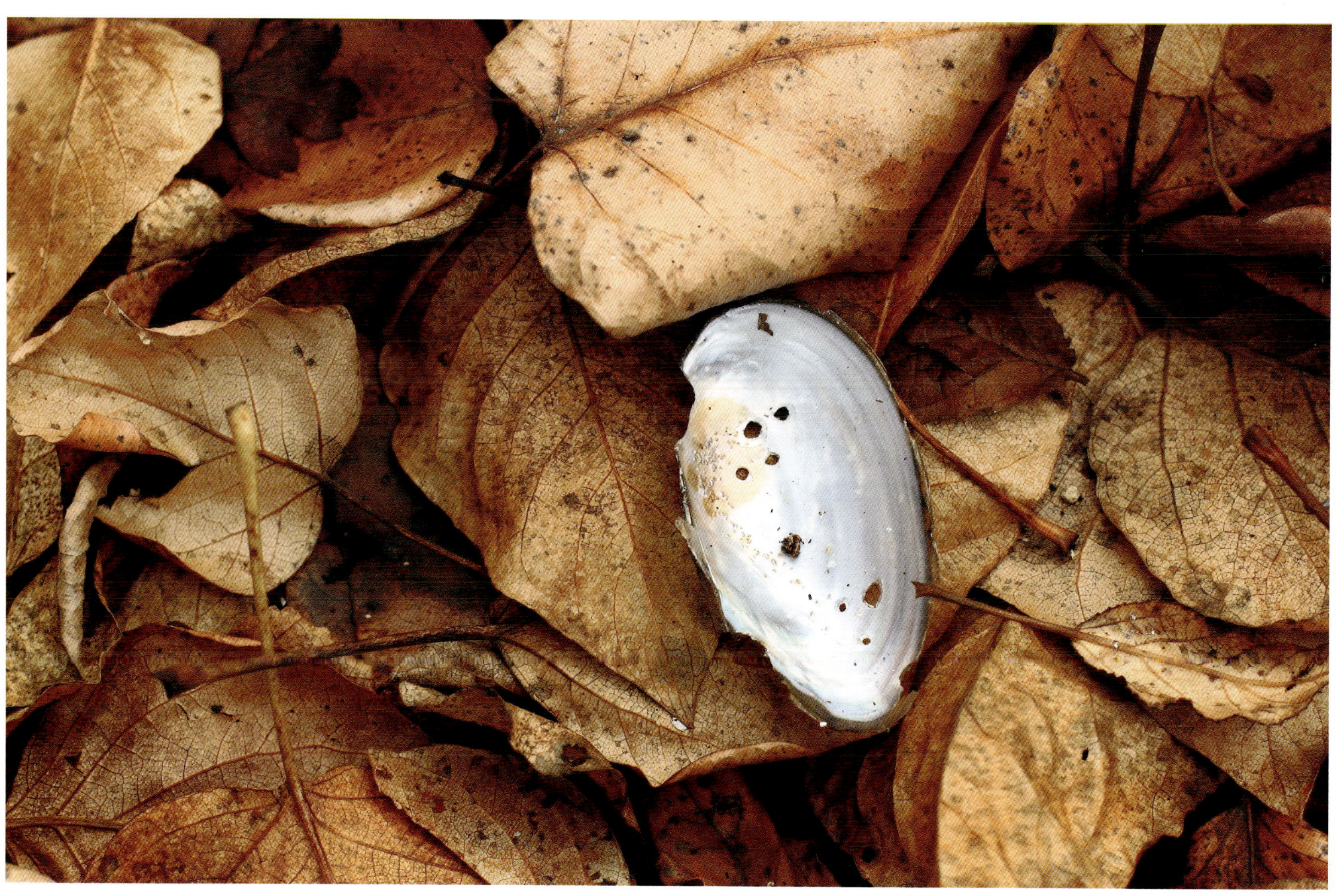

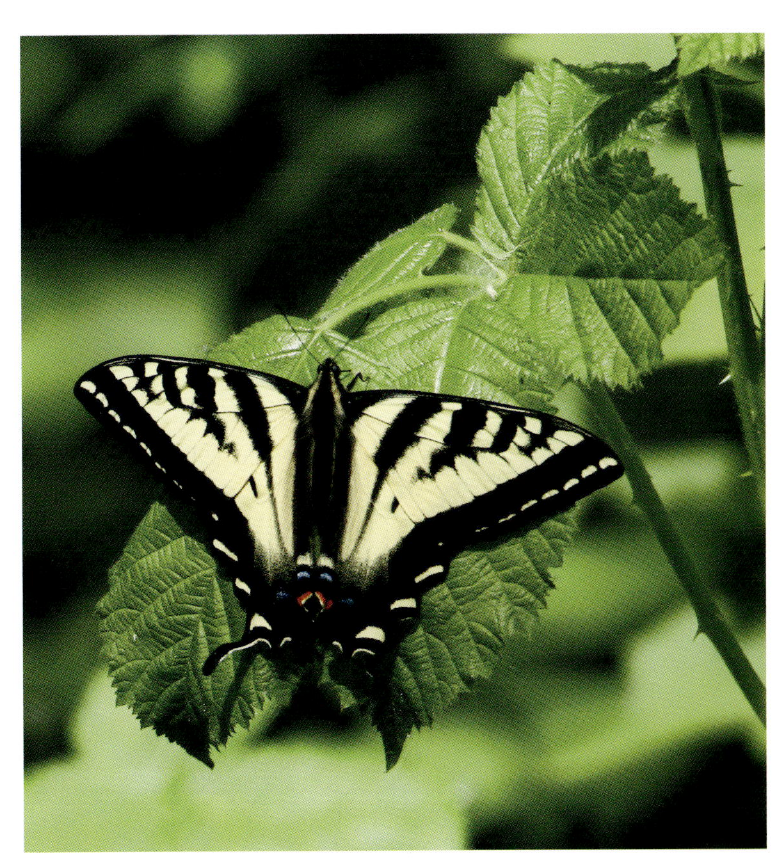

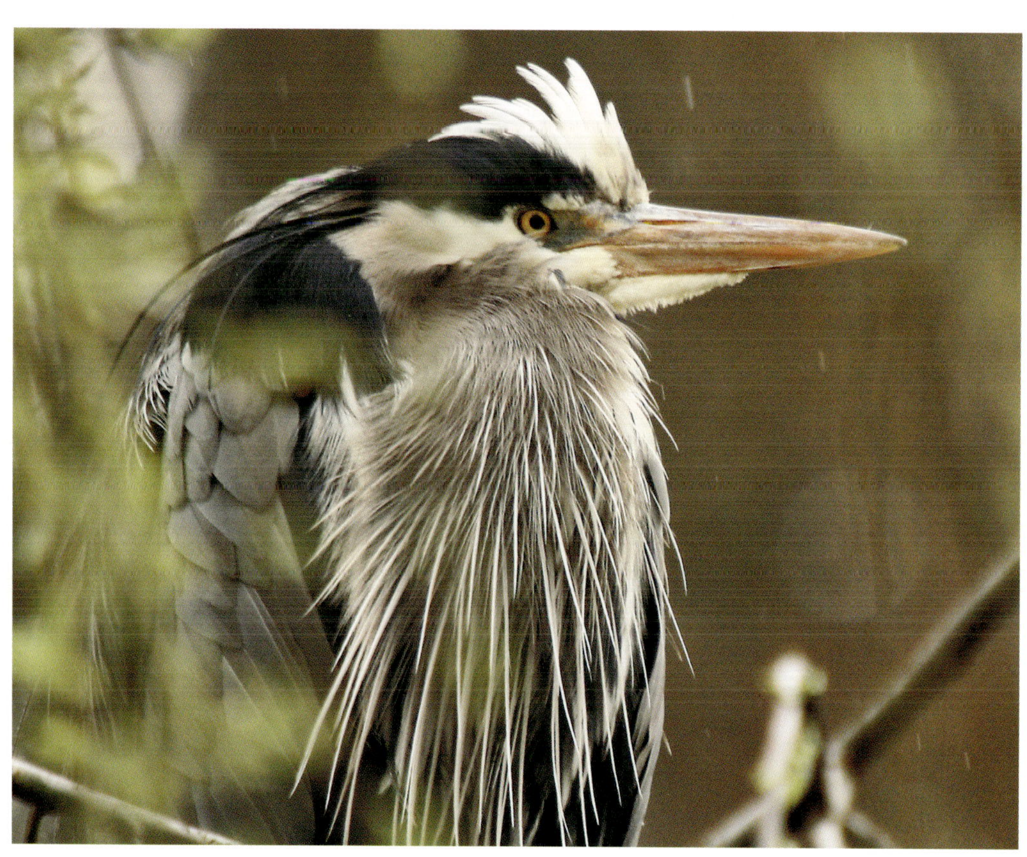

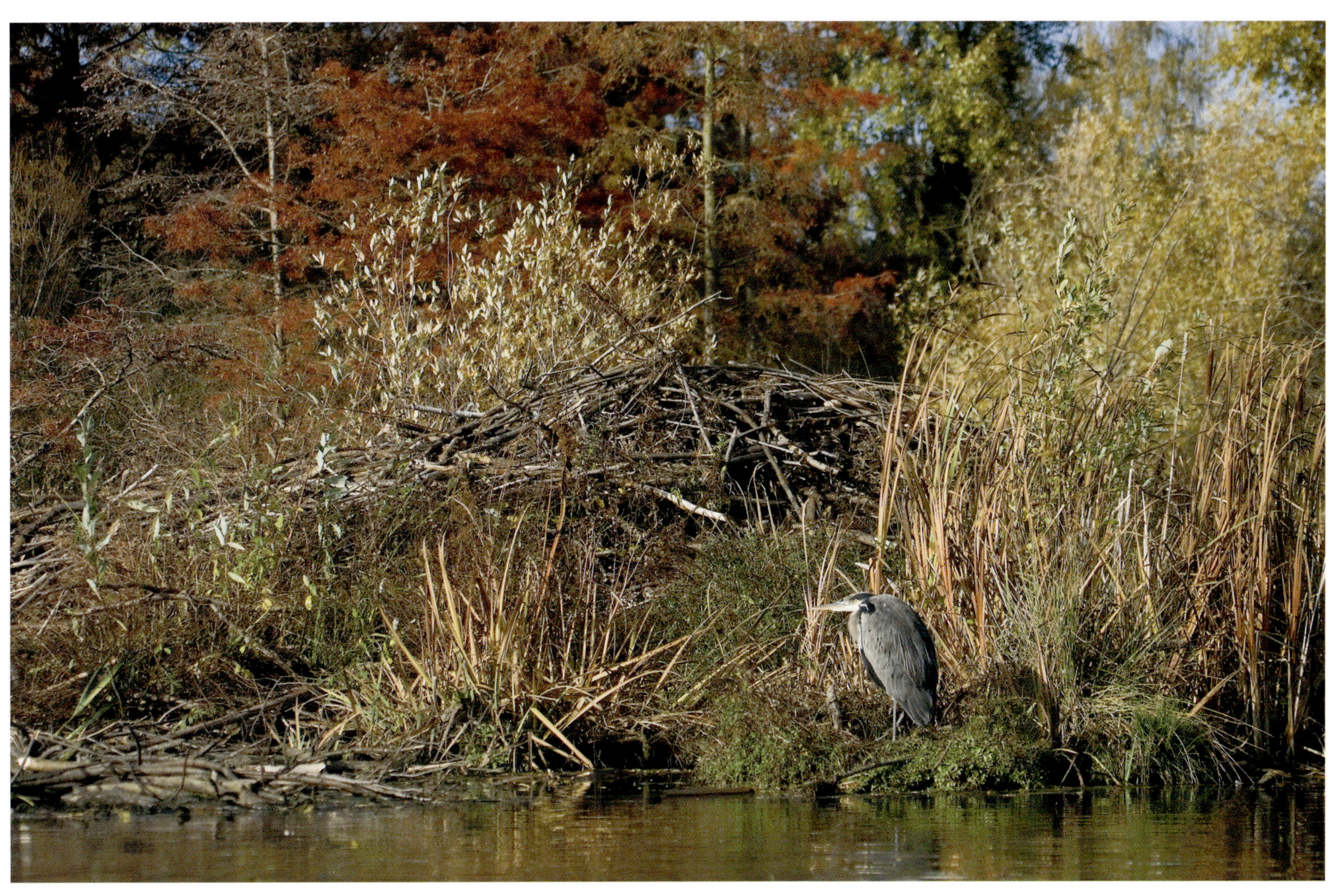

As a special place of wonderment, pleasure, and discovery, I have loved the Washington Park Arboretum since early boyhood. I grew up in the nearby Denny Blaine neighborhood, and our family often visited the Arboretum on weekends for bicycling along Arboretum Drive, exploring the miniature landscaping and artistry of the Japanese Tea Garden, swimming and fishing from Duck Bay and Foster Island in the wetlands, family picnics and Easter egg hunts (where real bunnies could be seen!) in the flats along Azalea Way, and just casual strolls on the many pleasant and rightful trails. And with so many secret paths, what a place for hide-and-seek—always a favorite of mine!

On the many visits to the Arboretum with my father, he would call attention to a particularly unusual tree or plant, and sometimes create a watercolor of the flowering azaleas or sketch lush landscape scenes while we happily played. To this day, I have a deep appreciation for the beauty of the collections and natural and cultivated landscapes found in the Arboretum and its wetlands, as well as for the educational, leisure, and recreational opportunities it provides.

Seattle just wouldn't be the same without the Arboretum. Having such an expansive natural setting of everything from rolling hills with a rich variety of trees and gardens to cattail-laced waterways in the heart of our city is truly a unique treasure for all. Thankfully, countless people in the community have fought against freeways and other threats to preserve and enhance this treasure. While institutions have been committed to the Arboretum for many years, these devotees have worked hard to make sure everyone has access to the same experiences I was lucky enough to have as a boy.

Now I have a family of my own, and we can still enjoy frequent visits and many of the same activities in the Arboretum, a special place of permanence through changing times.

— *Peter Steinbrueck, FAIA*

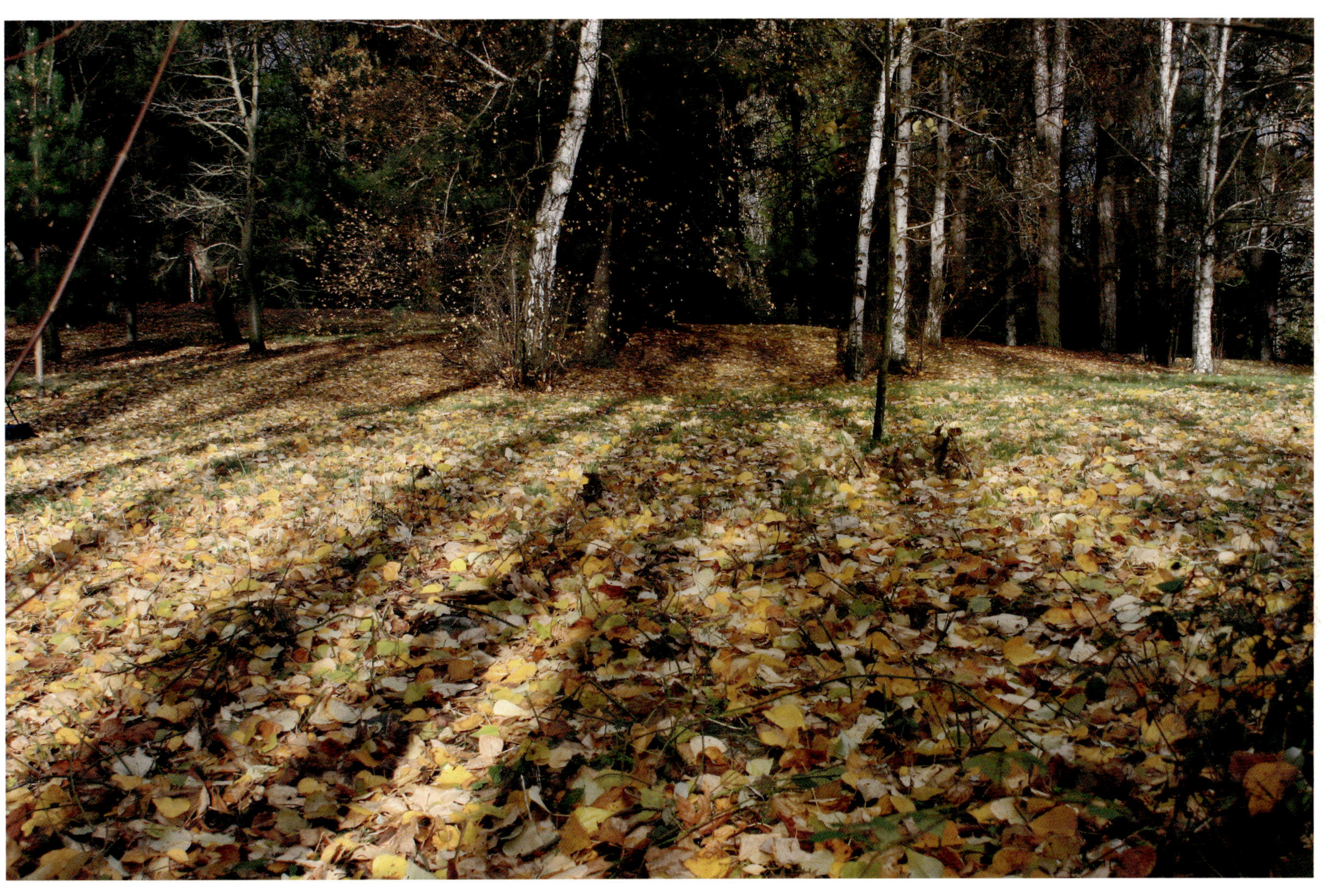

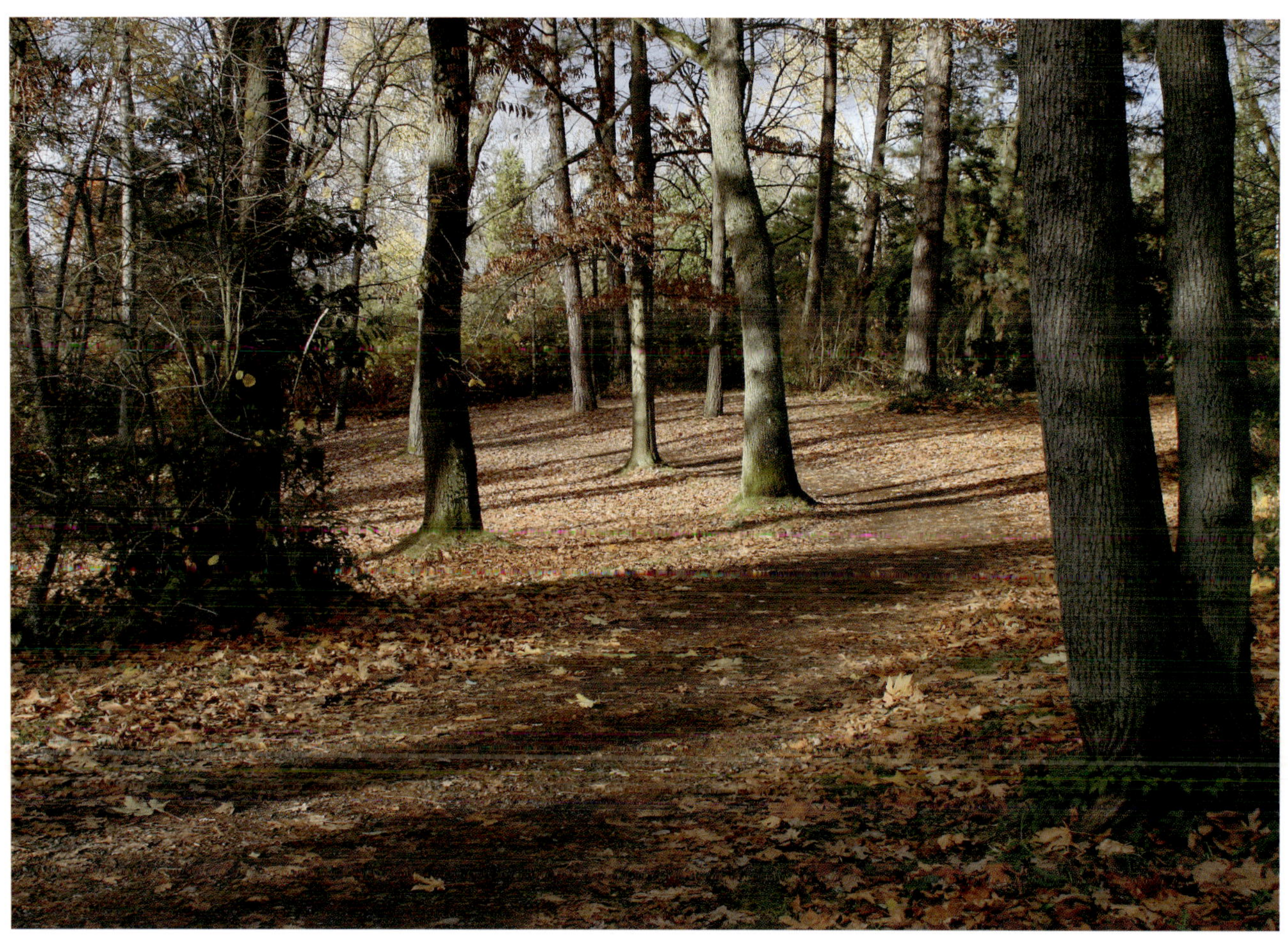

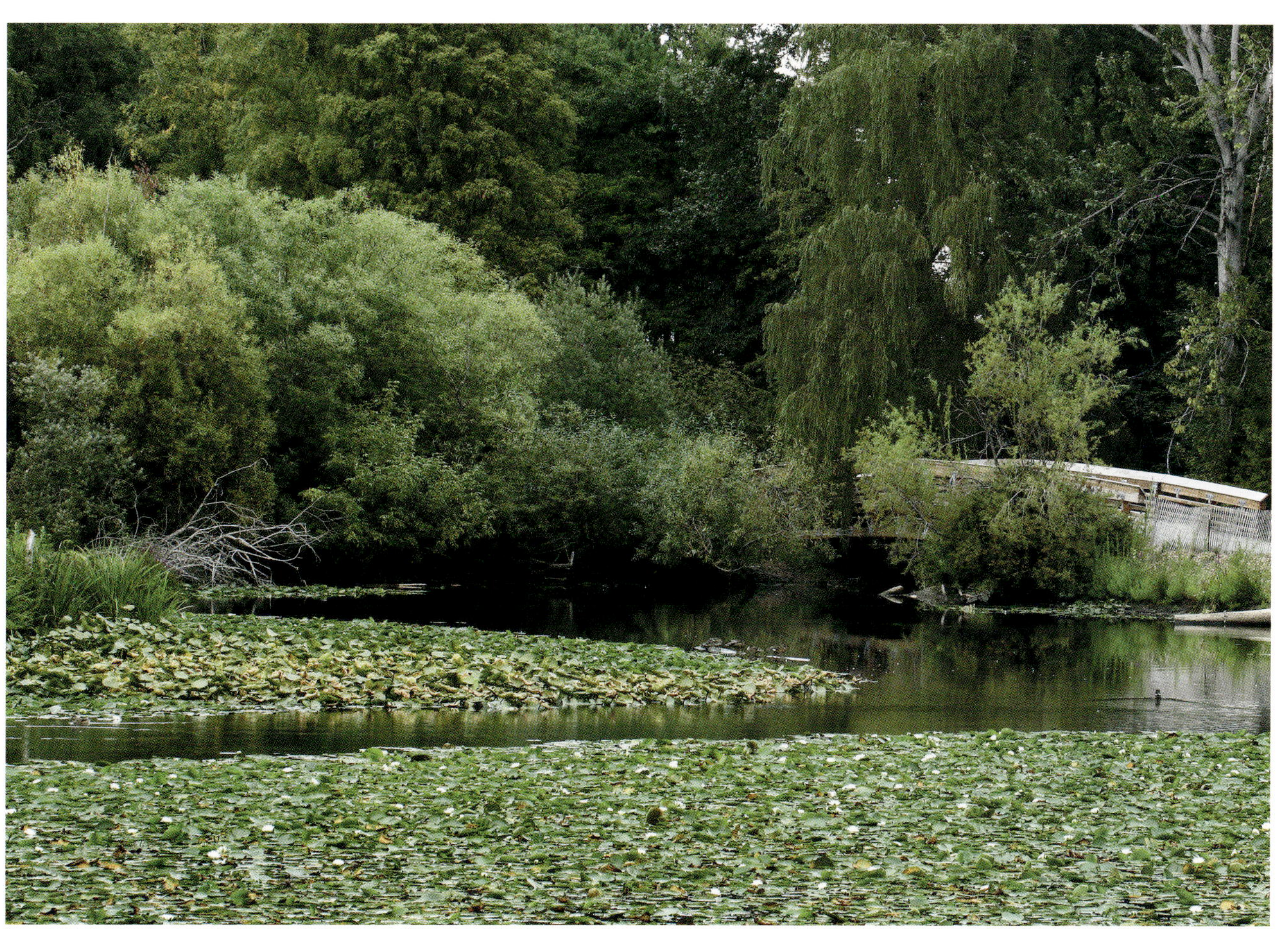

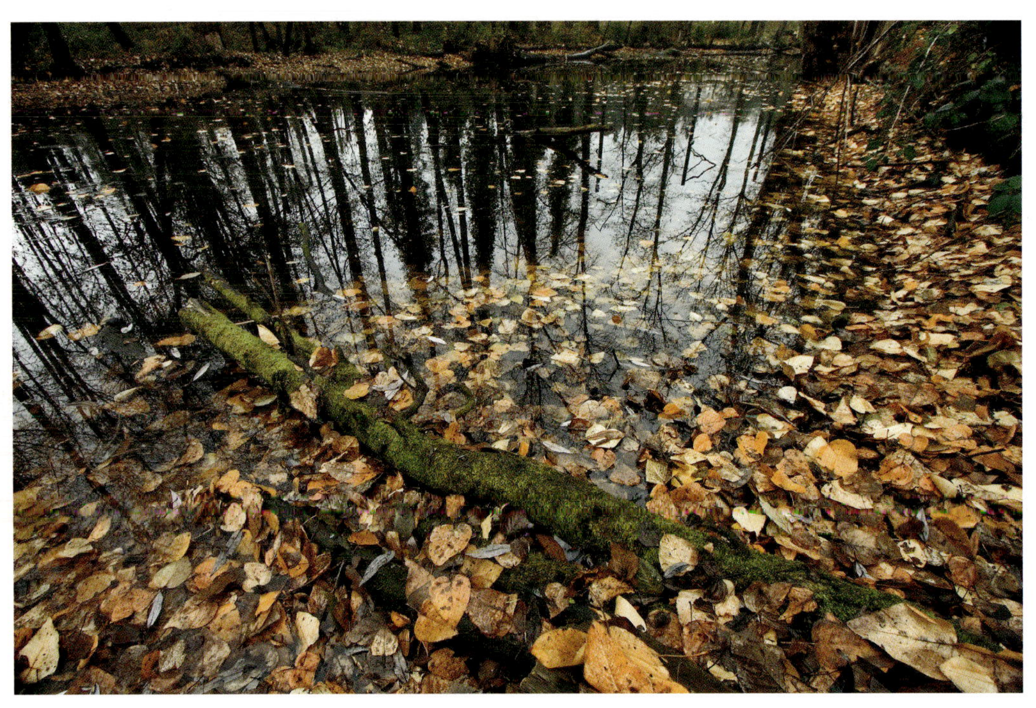

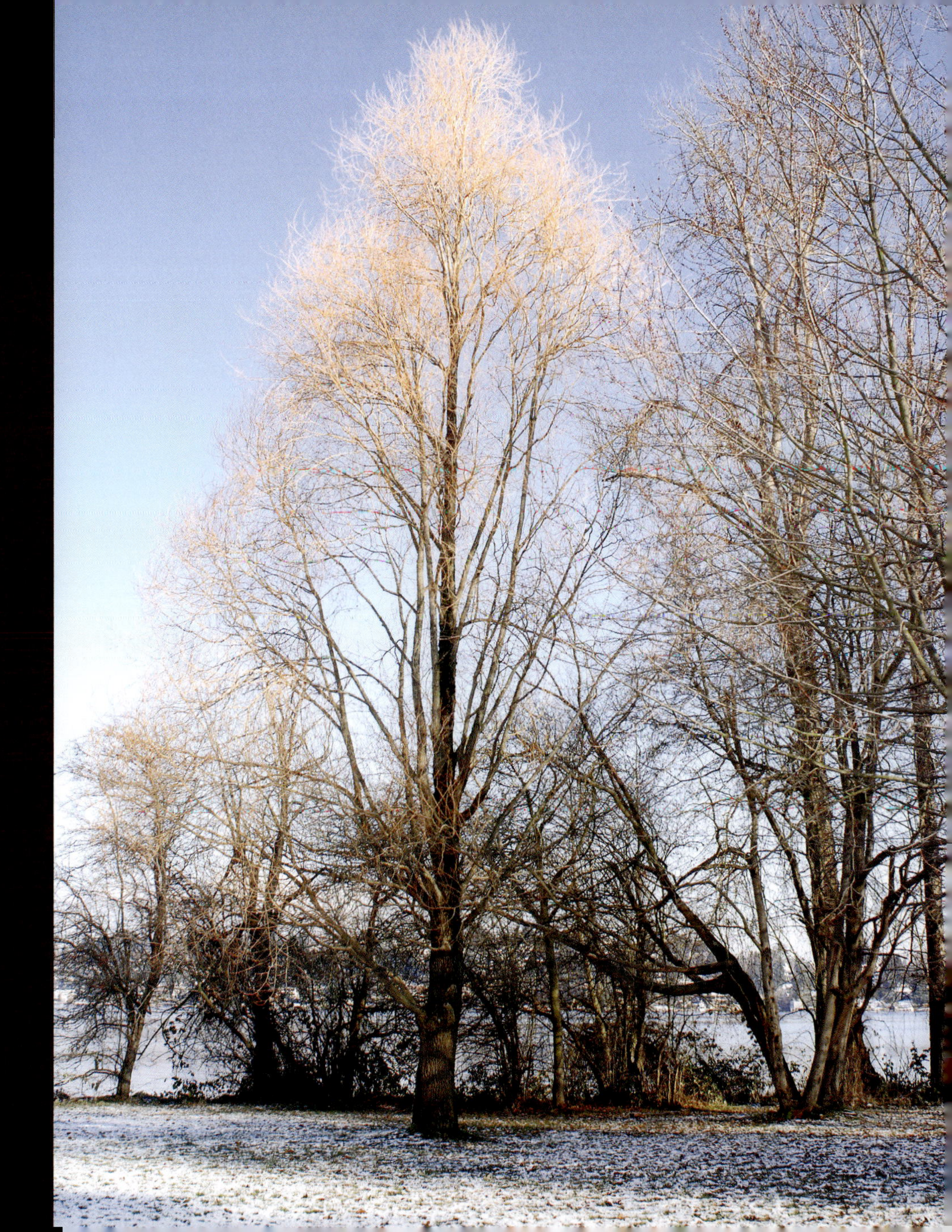

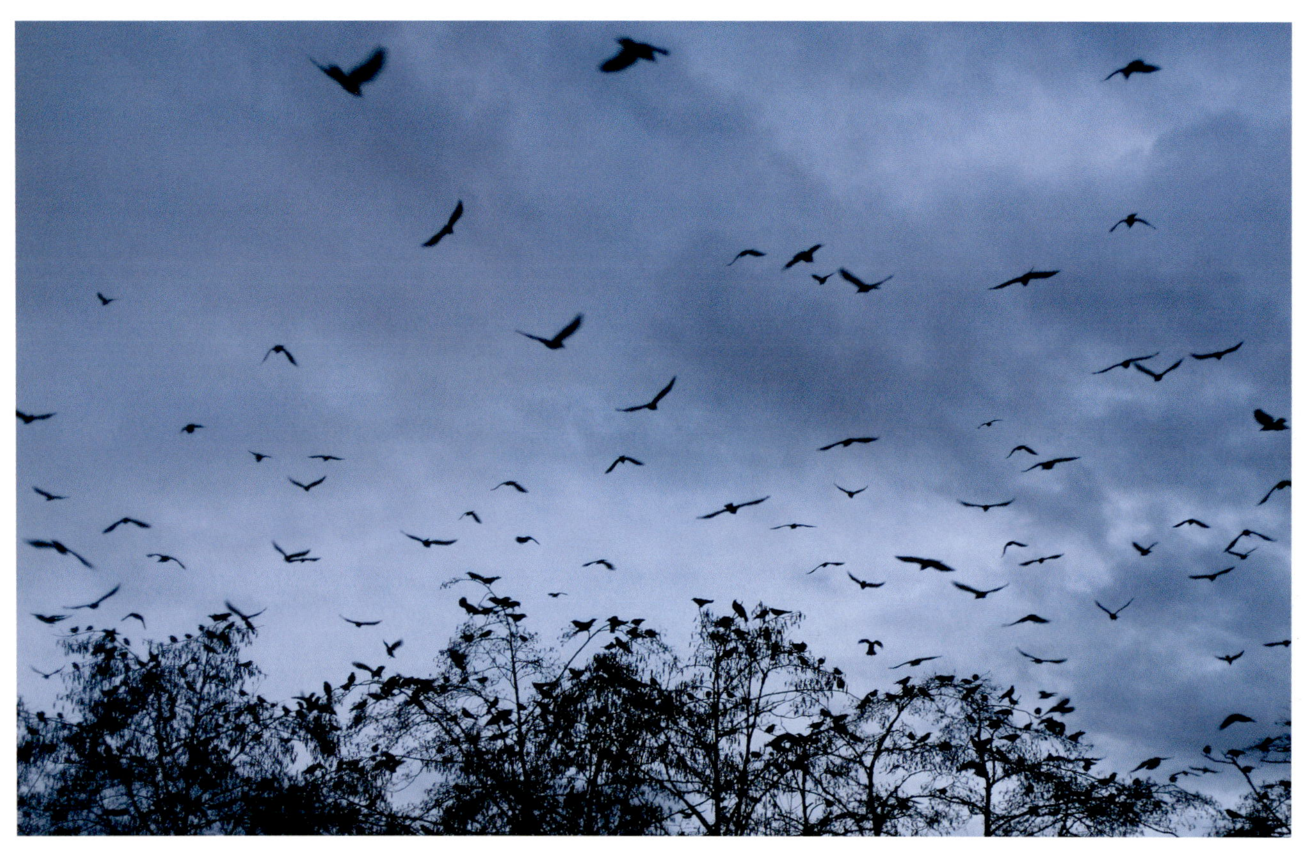

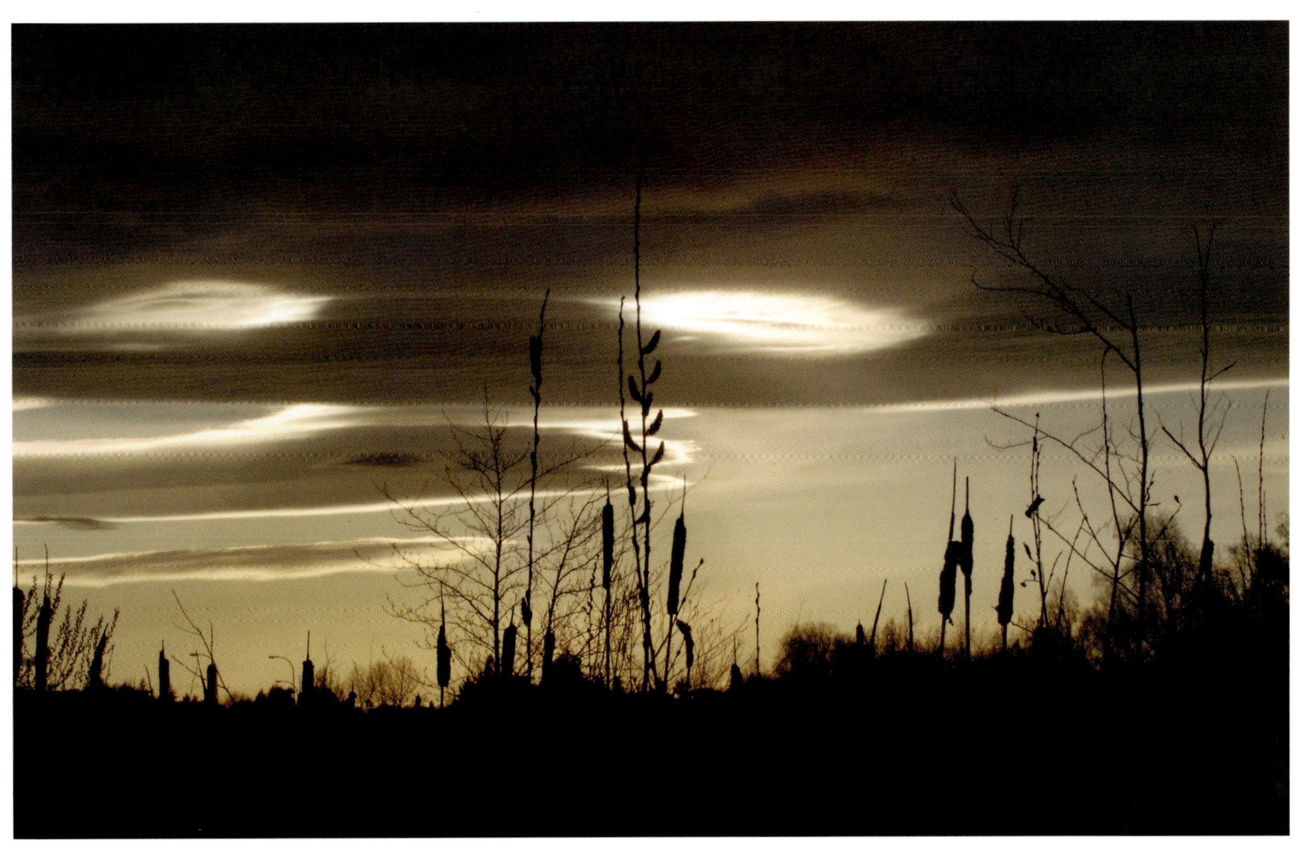

One thing we have learned over the last 50 years is that it is not possible to preserve enough places to sustain wild critters by attempting to exclude us humans from their habitat. It is estimated by the World Resources Institute, a respected environmental think tank, that worldwide, we have set aside about eight percent of the world's land to be forever wild. In practice, less than one percent really qualifies as wild because humans continue to encroach on those set-aside places.

Human pressures are not likely to decrease over the next 50 years. Our sheer numbers when coupled with traditional development patterns, increased wealth, and technological advances will bring additional human demand for land and the potential for crowding out wildlife.

Many things can be done about these trends, including increasing public knowledge of our impact on wild things and control over the patterns of our development.

A good start is to preserve and protect the examples of wild places and things we now have. Seattle's Arboretum wetlands are a case in point—a wild place in a densely urban setting.

As the beautiful, evocative photographs in this book illustrate, the Arboretum wetlands are an enchanting place. They are and should remain an educational tool and a reminder to all our citizens that wildlife can live and even thrive surrounded by us humans, if only we let them.

It is within our power to preserve these living things. It is unconscionable for us not to do it.

—William D. Ruckelshaus

First and Fifth Administrator of the United States Environmental Protection Agency

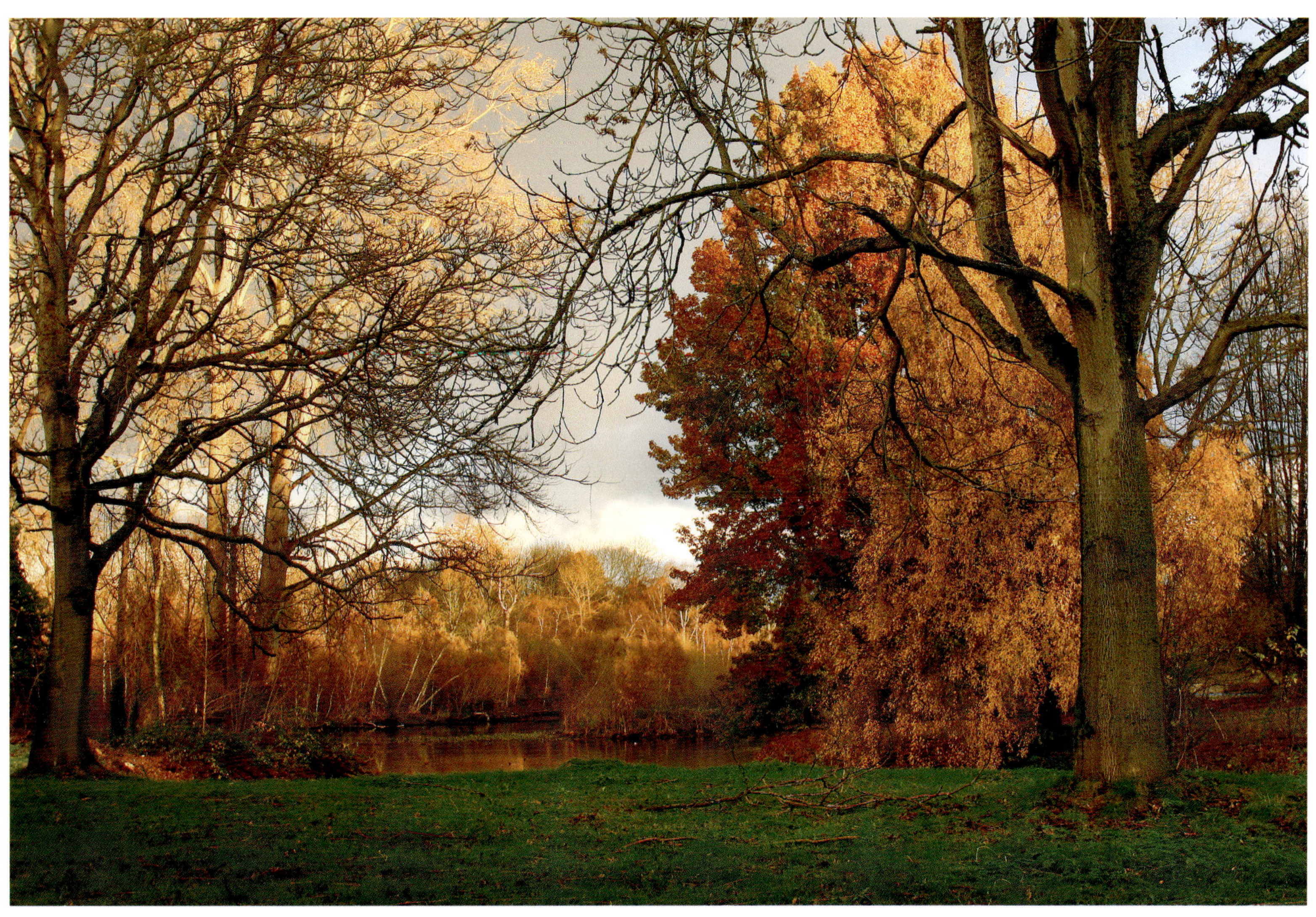

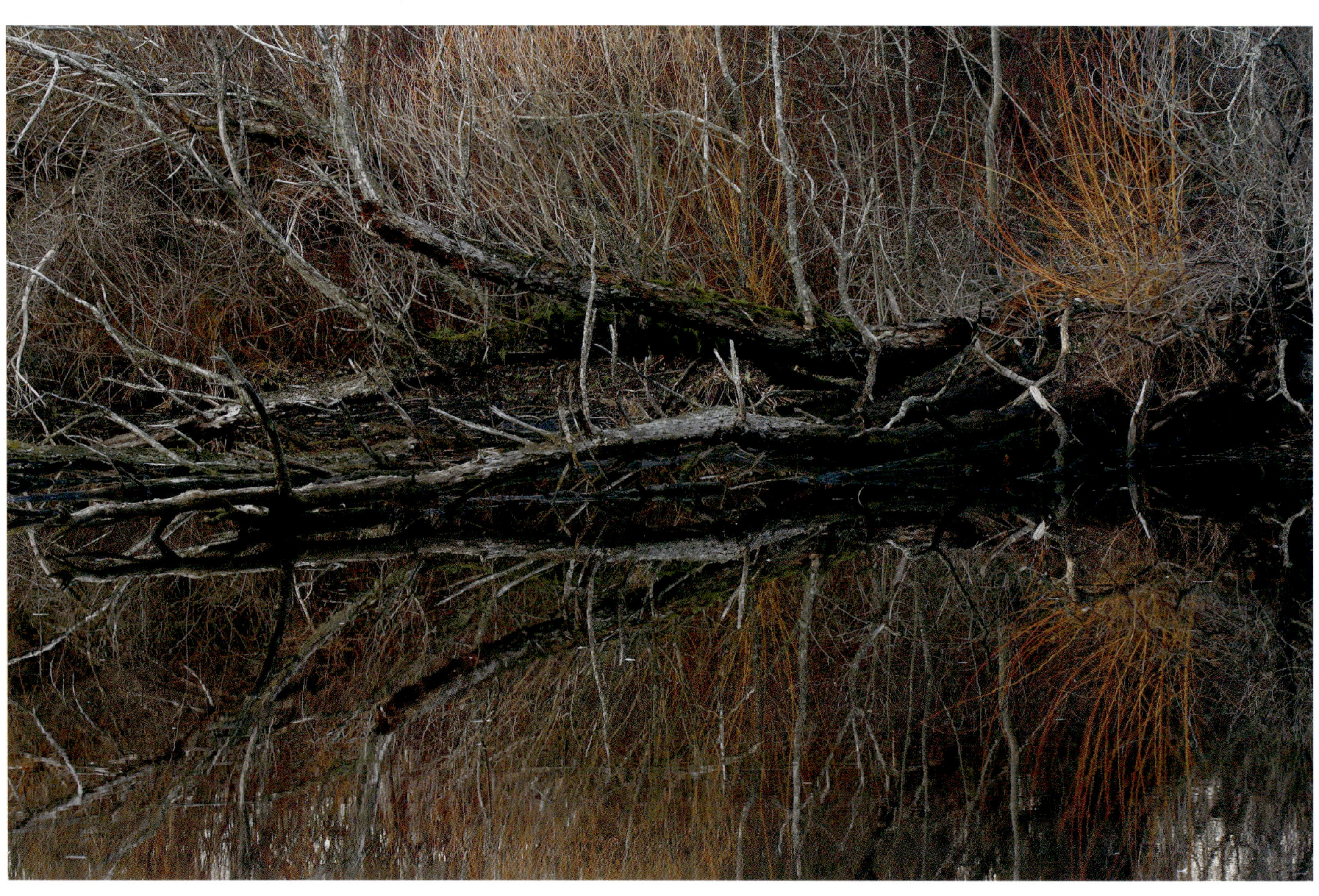

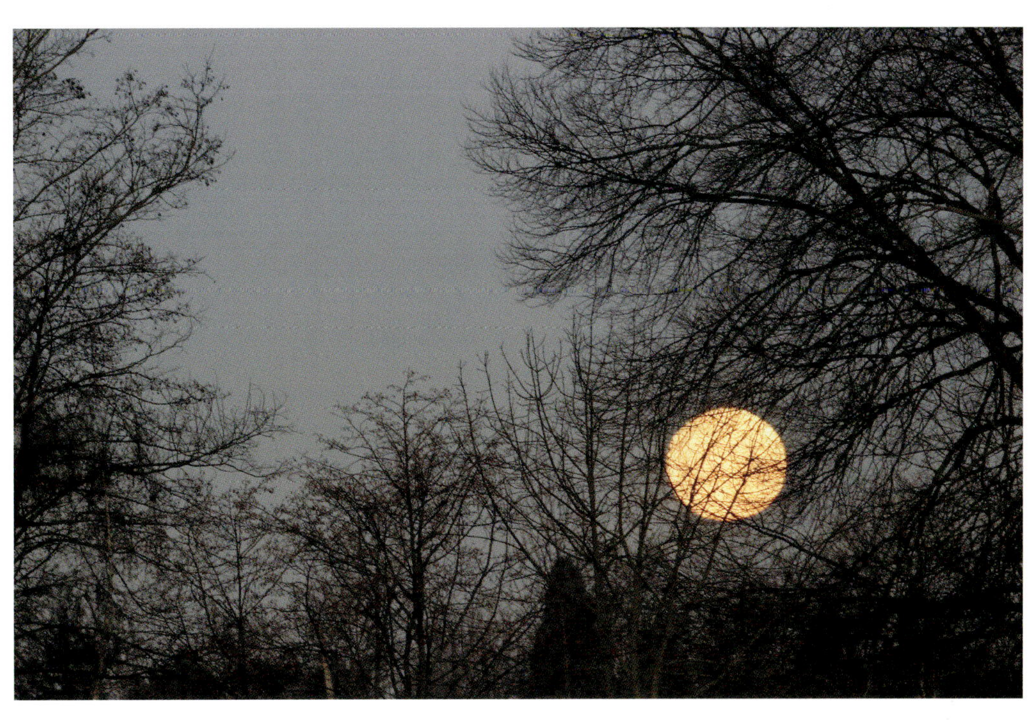

Index

Number	Photographer/Author	Description
Cover	Margret Maria Cordts	trees with moss
1	Michele A. Burton	Canada geese
2	Hilary Emmer	great blue heron
3	Michael and Lisa Anderson	Introduction
4	Maridee BonaDea	walkway in fog
5	Shannon Marie Sweeney	beaver lodge
6	Hilary Emmer	winter landscape
7	Maridee BonaDea	early morning marsh
8	Michele A. Burton	night landscape
9	Maridee BonaDea	sunrise through cattails
10	Shannon Marie Sweeney	Foster Island trail
11	Lisa P. Anderson	snowy landscape
12	Michele A. Burton	snowy landscape
13	David Richardson	morning landscape
14	Lisa P. Anderson	snowy cattails
15	Shannon Marie Sweeney	rushes
16	Michele A. Burton	water reflection
17	Michele A. Burton	fall landscape
18	Michele A. Burton	turtles and cattails
19	Michele A. Burton	night landscape
20	Newell J. Burton	autumn willow tree
21	Margret Maria Cordts	tree reflection
22	Jennifer Au	leaves in ice
23	Dale Chihuly	
24	Shannon Marie Sweeney	trees reflected
25	Michele A. Burton	water reflection
26	Michele A. Burton	water reflection
27	Marcia M. Mueller	mallard
28	Marcia M. Mueller	Douglas spirea
29	Lisa P. Anderson	European birch
30	Maridee BonaDea	cattails at sunrise
31	Marcia M. Mueller	water reflection
32	Kevin Ebi	white water lilies (introduced species)

Number	Photographer/Author	Description
33	Michele A. Burton	cottonwood leaf on duckweed
34	Michele A. Burton	yellow flag iris (introduced species)
35	Skye Boardman	white water lilies (introduced species)
36	Michele A. Burton	aquatic grass
37	John J. Taylor	water droplets on horsetails
38	Kevin Ebi	leaf on water
39	Peter Seligmann	
40	Michele A. Burton	cottonwood trees reflected
41	Kevin Ebi	great blue heron
42	Michele A. Burton	great blue heron
43	Michele A. Burton	green heron
44	Roger Hoesterey	
45	Michele A. Burton	great blue heron and irises in rain
46	Michele A. Burton	cottonwood seeds on water
47	Michele A. Burton	mallard with cottonwood seeds
48	Skye Boardman	pied-billed grebes
49	Michele A. Burton	wood duck ducklings
50	Michele A. Burton	pied-billed grebe (composite)
51	Robert Fulghum	
52	Camden Hackworth	wood duck
53	Michele A. Burton	painted turtles
54	Kevin Ebi	red-eared slider turtle (introduced species)
55	Michele A. Burton	eight-spotted skimmer
56	Skye Boardman	white water lily with damselflies
57	David Richardson	Virginia rail
58	Kevin Ebi	bullfrog
59	Michele A. Burton	
60	Michele A. Burton	great blue heron
61	Michele A. Burton	northern shoveler
62	Camden Hackworth	bufflehead
63	Camden Hackworth	northern shoveler
64	Camden Hackworth	hooded merganser
65	John J. Taylor	cinnamon teal
66	Michele A. Burton	American coots
67	Michele A. Burton	American coots
68	Camden Hackworth	American coots
69	Michele A. Burton	American coots
70	Michele A. Burton	American coots

Number	Photographer/Author	Description
71	Jennifer Leigh	mallards coming in for a landing
72	Camden Hackworth	gadwall
73	Camden Hackworth	wood duck
74	Michele A. Burton	nutria (introduced species)
75	Michele A. Burton	nutria (introduced species)
76	Edward Gee	barred owl
77	John J. Taylor	raccoon
78	Michele A. Burton	paper wasp nest
79	Joan Burton	
80	Lisa P. Anderson	Canada goose and great blue heron
81	Michele A. Burton	beaver
82	Camden Hackworth	bald eagle
83	Raymond Parsons	bald eagle
84	Rob Jones III	bald eagle
85	Lisa P. Anderson	bald eagle
86	Marcia M. Mueller	
87	Michele A. Burton	marsh wren
88	Michele A. Burton	red-winged blackbird (composite)
89	Jennifer Leigh	Anna's hummingbird
90-93	Michele A. Burton	barn swallows
94	Michele A. Burton	brown creeper
95	Michele A. Burton	northern flicker
96	Michele A. Burton	cedar waxwing
97	John J. Taylor	American goldfinch
98	Raymond Parsons	cedar waxwing
99	Lisa P. Anderson	European bittersweet berries
100	Newell J. Burton	iris seeds
101	Michele A. Burton	Himalayan blackberry (invasive species) on poplar tree
102	Rodney Pond	
103	Shannon Marie Sweeney	elm tree trunks
104	David Richardson	spiders in web
105	Maridee BonaDea	grass abstract
106	Dan Evans	
107	Jennifer Au	mushrooms
108	Michele A. Burton	Salix babylonica "crispa" (non-native)
109	Margret Maria Cordts	native lily
110	Michele A. Burton	Steller's jay

Number	Photographer/Author	Description
111	Jennifer Leigh	Japanese maple
112	Marcia M. Mueller	yellow willow
113	Lisa P. Anderson	branches
114	Michele A. Burton	freshwater clam on cottonwood leaves
115	Michele A. Burton	western tiger swallowtail
116	Camden Hackworth	great blue heron
117	Michele A. Burton	great blue heron and beaver lodge
118	Peter Steinbrueck	
119	Newell J. Burton	fall landscape
120	Newell J. Burton	fall landscape
121	Michele A. Burton	summer landscape
122	Margret Maria Cordts	December trees reflected
123	Shannon Marie Sweeney	snowy landscape
124	Michele A. Burton	American crows
125	Rob Jones III	sunrise through cattails
126	William D. Ruckelshaus	
127	Michele A. Burton	fall sunset
128	Michele A. Burton	fall landscape
129	David Richardson	winter moonrise
130	Michele A. Burton	belted kingfisher
Back Cover	Kevin Ebi	great blue heron

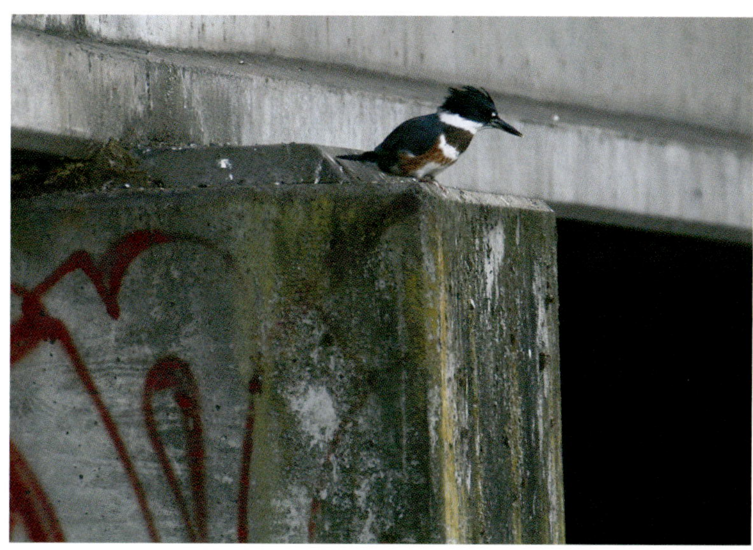

THE WILD WITHIN

Wetlands of the Washington Park Arboretum

Published by Documentary Media
3250 41st Ave SW
Seattle, WA 98116

www.documentarymedia.com
books@docbooks.com
(206) 935-9292

First edition 2007
Printed in China

Special thanks to all of the photographers and writers who submitted work to this book project, whether or not it ended up in the final draft. We are inspired by your contributions, unique perspectives, and obvious love of these wetlands.

Producers: Michael and Lisa Anderson
Sponsor: Wetland Alliance, LLC
Essays: Joan Burton, Michele A. Burton, Dale Chihuly, Dan Evans, Robert Fulghum, Roger Hoesterey, Marcia M. Mueller, Rodney Pond, William D. Ruckelshaus, Peter Seligmann, and Peter Steinbrueck
Photography: Lisa P. Anderson, Jennifer Au, Skye Boardman, Maridee BonaDea, Michele A. Burton, Newell J. Burton, Margret Maria Cordts, Kevin Ebi, Hilary Emmer, Edward Gee, Camden Hackworth, Rob Jones III, Jennifer Leigh, Marcia M. Mueller, Raymond Parsons, David Richardson, Shannon Marie Sweeney, and John J. Taylor

Publisher: Barry Provorse
Editorial Director: Petyr Beck
Editor: Judy Gouldthorpe
Photo Editor: Marc Shor, Barn Door Productions
Photo Management Services: SmugMug
Nature Editor: Dale Herter, wildlife biologist, Raedeke Associates, Inc.

Book Design: Paul Langland Design

Library of Congress Cataloging-in-Publication Data
The wild within : wetlands of the Washington Park Arboretum / essays by Joan Burton ... [et al.] ; photography, Lisa P. Anderson ... [et al.]. — 1st ed.
p. cm.

ISBN 978-1-933245-09-6
1. Nature photography—Washington (State) 2. Wetlands—Washington (State)—Pictorial works.
3. Washington Park Arboretum—Pictorial works. I. Burton, Joan, 1935- II. Anderson, Lisa P.

TR721.W49 2007
779'.309797772—dc22
2007028232